OFFICIAL SQA PAST PAPERS WITH SQA ANSWERS

Higher
HUMAN BIOLOGY

Higher Grade 1998 to 1999, and Higher Still Specimen Question Paper, 2000 and 2001 with three years' answers

© Copyright Scottish Qualifications Authority

First exam published in 1998.

Published by
Leckie & Leckie Ltd, 8 Whitehill Terrace, St. Andrews, Scotland KY16 8RN
tel: 01334 475656 fax: 01334 477392
hq@leckieandleckie.co.uk www.leckieandleckie.co.uk

Leckie & Leckie Project Management Team: Tom Davie; David Nicoll; Bruce Ryan
Cover Design Assistance: Mike Middleton

ISBN 1-84372-010-8

A CIP Catalogue record for this book is available from the British Library.

Printed in Scotland by Inglis Allen on environmentally friendly paper. The paper is made from a mixture of sawmill waste, forest thinnings and wood from sustainable forests.

® Leckie & Leckie is a registered trademark.

Leckie & Leckie Ltd achieved the Investors in People Standard in 1999.

INVESTOR IN PEOPLE

Leckie & Leckie

Introduction

The best way to prepare for exams is to practise, again and again, all that you have learned over the past year. Work through these questions and check your solutions against these *official SQA answers*. But give yourself a real chance and be honest! Make sure you work through each question thoroughly so that you understand how you got the right answer – *you will have to do this in the exam*!

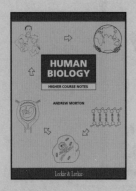

Higher Human Biology Course Notes. These accessible course notes provide lucid explanations to often highly complex, technical matters. Bold print empasises key words which are clearly explained by context or definition.

Questions in Higher Human Biology. An excellent crop of questions across the subject field. Develop your exam technique with the practice exam paper, then check your answers with our special pull-out answer section.

Contents

Leckie & Leckie has made every effort to trace all copyright holders. If any have been inadvertently overlooked, Leckie & Leckie will be pleased to make the necessary arrangements.

FOR OFFICIAL USE

Presenting Centre No.	Subject No.	Level	Paper No.	Group No.	Marker's No.
	1800	**H**	**2**		

Total

1800/202

SCOTTISH
CERTIFICATE OF
EDUCATION
1998

MONDAY, 11 MAY
9.30 AM – 12.00 NOON

HUMAN BIOLOGY
HIGHER GRADE
Paper II

Fill in these boxes and read what is printed below.

Full name of school or college

Town

First name and initials

Surname

Date of birth
Day Month Year   Candidate number   Number of seat

1 (a)   All questions should be attempted.

   (b)   **Question 10 is on pages 16, 17 and 18 and Question 11 is on pages 19, 20 and 21—pages 18 and 19 are fold-out pages.**

   (c)   It should be noted that questions 13 and 14 each contain a choice.

2 The questions may be answered in any order but all answers are to be written in the spaces provided in this answer book, and must be written clearly and legibly in ink.

3 Additional space for answers and rough work will be found at the end of the book. If further space is required, supplementary sheets may be obtained from the invigilator and should be inserted inside the **front** cover of this booklet.

4 The numbers of questions must be clearly inserted with any answers written in the additional space.

5 Rough work, if any should be necessary, should be written in this booklet and then scored through when the fair copy has been written.

6 Before leaving the examination room you must give this book to the invigilator. If you do not, you may lose all the marks for this paper.

SCOTTISH
QUALIFICATIONS
AUTHORITY

SECTION A

All questions in this section should be attempted.

Marks

1. The diagram below represents a cell involved in the synthesis and secretion of pepsin.

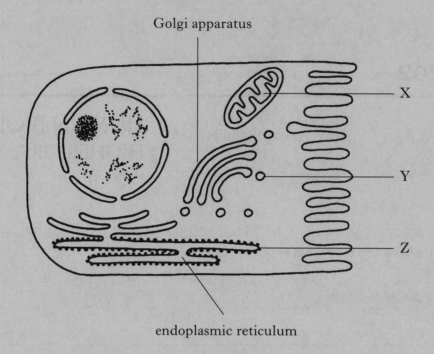

Golgi apparatus

endoplasmic reticulum

(a) Complete the table by giving the names and functions of organelles X, Y and Z involved in this process.

Label	Name	Function
X		
Y		
Z		

(3)

Marks

1. **(continued)**

   (b) (i) What feature of DNA ensures that amino acids are linked in the correct order to synthesise pepsin?

   _____

   _____ **(1)**

   (ii) Describe the roles of mRNA and tRNA in the synthesis of pepsin.

   mRNA _____

   _____

   _____

   _____

   tRNA _____

   _____

   _____

   _____ **(2)**

   (c) Complete the following sentences by **<u>underlining</u>** the correct alternatives.

   The enzyme pepsin is secreted into the $\begin{cases} \text{duodenum} \\ \text{stomach} \\ \text{colon} \end{cases}$ and its substrate is $\begin{cases} \text{protein} \\ \text{starch} \\ \text{fat} \end{cases}$.

   The optimum pH for pepsin is $\begin{cases} 2 \\ 7 \\ 9 \end{cases}$ and the products of digestion are $\begin{cases} \text{sugar} \\ \text{fatty acids} \\ \text{peptides} \end{cases}$. **(2)**

   [Turn over

2. The diagram below represents part of the plasma membrane of a red blood cell *Marks* which is passing through a blood capillary in a muscle.

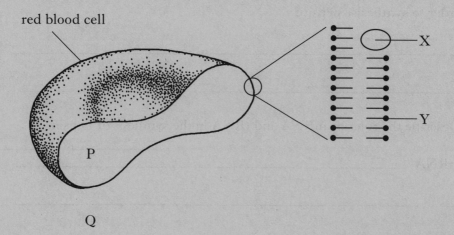

(a) Name molecules X and Y.

X _____   Y _____ **(1)**

(b) Why is the arrangement of molecules in the membrane often described as a fluid mosaic?

_____

_____

_____ **(2)**

(c) State a possible function of molecule X.

_____

_____ **(1)**

(d) Draw an arrow on the diagram between points P and Q to indicate the direction of diffusion of oxygen across the membrane of the red blood cell. **(1)**

(e) (i) The solute concentration of blood plasma is kept within narrow limits. How does this ensure that red blood cells maintain their biconcave shape?

_____

_____

_____ **(1)**

Candidates must not write in this margin

Marks

2. (*e*) (continued)

(ii) Explain the significance of the biconcave shape of red blood cells.

____

____

______________________________ **(1)**

(iii) Name the pituitary secretion which controls the solute concentration of the blood plasma.

______________________________ **(1)**

(iv) Name **two** solutes found in blood plasma.

1 ______________ 2 ______________ **(1)**

[Turn over

3. The diagram below represents the primary humoral immune response following a viral invasion.

Marks

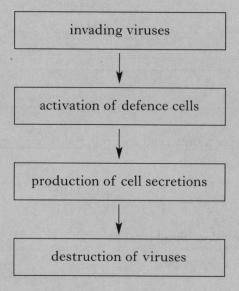

(a) (i) Name the defence cells which are mobilised during the humoral response.

_____   **(1)**

(ii) What feature of the invading virus is recognised by the defence cells?

_____   **(1)**

(iii) Name the cell secretions which destroy viruses.

_____   **(1)**

(b) If the same virus invades the body again, a secondary humoral immune response occurs. How does this response differ from the primary response?

_____

_____   **(1)**

(c) After invasion, viruses cause body cells to produce new viruses. Name **two** molecules provided by body cells which are required for the construction of new viral DNA.

1 _____

2 _____   **(2)**

4. The diagrams below show two human cells in which nuclear division is taking place. Only some of the chromosomes are shown.

Marks

       Cell A   Cell B

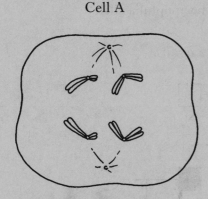 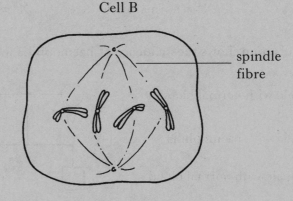

                        spindle
                        fibre

(a)   (i)   In which cell is meiosis taking place? Give a reason for your answer.

     Cell _____

     Reason _____

     _____ **(1)**

  (ii)   Describe the stage of nuclear division shown in each diagram.

     Cell A _____

     _____

     Cell B _____

     _____ **(2)**

  (iii)   How many chromatids are visible in cell B?

     _____ **(1)**

(b)   What terms are used to describe the chromosome complement of the daughter cells formed after each division process is complete?

     Cell A _____

     Cell B _____ **(1)**

[Turn over

Marks

5. Haemophilia is a sex-linked condition in which the blood does not clot normally. The alleles are represented using the following symbols.

$$X^H = \text{normal allele} \qquad X^h = \text{haemophilia allele}$$

The diagram shows the incidence of haemophilia in a family.

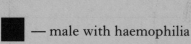 — male with normal blood

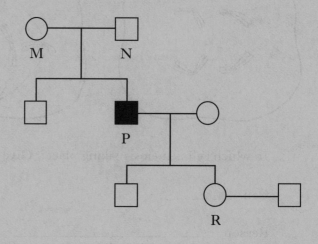

— male with haemophilia

— female with normal blood

(a) Where are sex-linked genes found?

_____ **(1)**

(b) State the genotypes of individuals M, N and P.

M _____

N _____

P _____   **(1)**

(c) Granddaughter R and her husband intend to have children, and seek genetic counselling.

(i) What information should be given to granddaughter R about the possibility of her inheritance of the allele for haemophilia?

_____

_____

_____ **(1)**

Marks

5. **(c) (continued)**

(ii) What information should be given to the husband of granddaughter R about the possibility of his inheritance of the allele for haemophilia? His father has haemophilia.

_____

_____

_____ **(1)**

(iii) What information should they be given about any children they might have?

_____

_____

_____

_____ **(2)**

(d) Name another sex-linked condition of humans.

_____ **(1)**

[Turn over

6. The table below refers to semen samples taken from five men.

Marks

Semen sample	A	B	C	D	E
Number of sperm in sample (millions/cm^3)	40	19	25	45	90
Active sperm (percent)	65	60	75	10	70
Abnormal sperm (percent)	30	20	90	30	10

(*a*) Name **two** glands involved in the production of semen.

_____ and _____ **(1)**

(*b*) A man is fertile if his semen contains at least 20 million sperm per/cm^3 and at least 60% of the sperm are both active and normal.

   (i) Which of the samples were taken from infertile men?

   _____ **(2)**

   (ii) Describe **one** treatment which could restore fertility to those men.

   _____

   _____ **(1)**

(*c*) Describe **one** cause of infertility in women.

_____

_____ **(1)**

(*d*) Infertility in women is sometimes treated using *in vitro* fertilisation. What is meant by the term "*in vitro* fertilisation"?

_____

_____ **(1)**

Candidates must not write in this margin

Marks

7. The behaviour of individuals is affected by the presence of others.

(*a*) Complete the table below by matching the type of behaviour with its definition.

Choose your answers from the list in the box.

social facilitation	**shaping**	**identification**
generalisation	**internalisation**	

Type of behaviour	*Definition*
	Process by which a desired behaviour is obtained as a result of training.
	Process by which an individual's performance is enhanced in a competitive situation.
	Process by which an individual changes his beliefs to be like another whom he admires.

(2)

(*b*) An individual may show a type of behaviour called deindividuation.

(i) Under what circumstances might this type of behaviour occur?

____

____

______________________________ **(1)**

(ii) Describe **one** feature of this type of behaviour.

____

____

______________________________ **(1)**

[Turn over

Marks

8. The diagram below shows the sequence of events during a cardiac cycle.

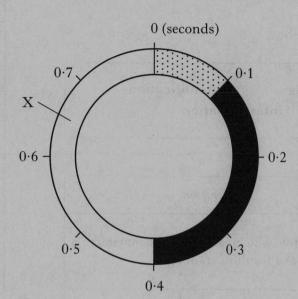

Stage	Key
X	
atrial systole	
ventricular systole	

(a) (i) Describe what happens to the heart during atrial systole.

_____

_____ **(1)**

     (ii) What causes atrial systole to occur?

_____

_____ **(1)**

(b) Name stage X.

_____ **(1)**

(c) (i) Between which two times in this cycle would blood flow in the aorta be at a maximum?

_____ and _____ (seconds) **(1)**

     (ii) At what time in this cycle will the semi-lunar valves close?

_____ **(1)**

Marks

8.   (continued)

(*d*)   Calculate the heart rate from the information in the diagram.

Space for calculation

_____ beats per minute   **(1)**

(*e*)   Name the **two** branches of the autonomic nervous system and state the effect of each branch on heart rate.

_____

_____

_____

_____

_____

_____   **(2)**

[Turn over

Marks

9. The diagram below shows the carbon cycle.

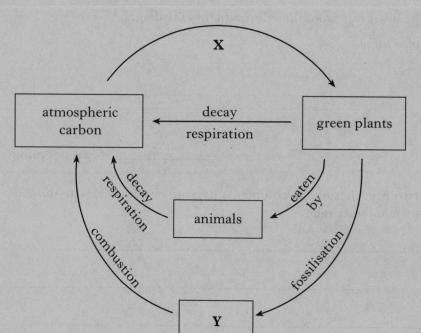

(a) (i) What process is indicated by the arrow at **X**?

_____ **(1)**

(ii) Describe **two** effects of this process on the composition of the atmosphere.

1 _____

2 _____ **(1)**

(iii) Suggest **two** substances which could be entered in box **Y**.

1 _____

2 _____ **(1)**

(b) (i) Give **two** reasons for the considerable increase in carbon dioxide concentrations in the atmosphere this century.

1 _____

_____

2 _____

_____ **(1)**

Marks

9. (b) (continued)

(ii) Increasing concentrations of carbon dioxide may cause global warming. Describe **two** possible consequences of global warming on world food production.

1 _____

_____

_____

2 _____

_____

_____ **(2)**

(c) Methane concentrations in the atmosphere are also increasing. Give a possible reason for this increase.

_____

_____

_____ **(1)**

[Turn over for Question 10 on pages *sixteen*, *seventeen* and *eighteen*.]

SECTION B

All questions in this section should be attempted.

10. This question relates to the ageing process.

Figure 1

Changes in resting metabolic rate with age

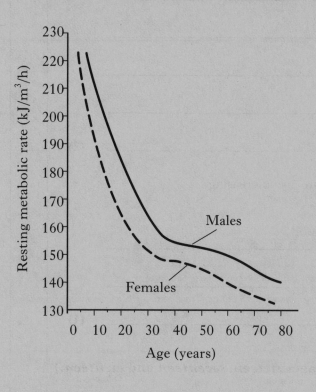

Figure 2

Changes in body tissue composition with age

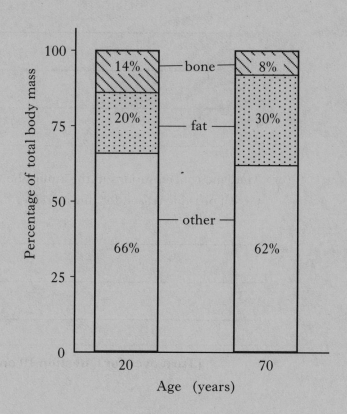

Figure 3

Changes in protein requirement with age

Age (years)	Average daily protein required (g/kg body mass)	Average body mass (kg)
8	1·5	28
20	0·8	75
70	0·6	70

Figure 4

Changes in bone density with age

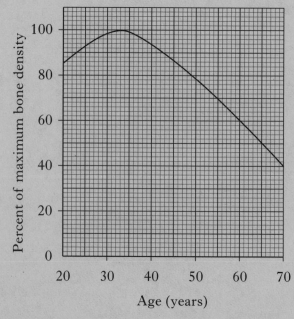

Question 10 continues on pages *seventeen* and the fold-out page *eighteen*

Marks

10. **(continued)**

    (*a*) Describe **two** general trends in resting metabolic rate shown by the graphs in **Figure 1**.

       1 _____

        _____

       2 _____

        _____ **(1)**

    (*b*) (i) With reference to **Figures 1** and **2**, state the relationship between resting metabolic rate and fat tissue content of the body with age.

            _____

            _____ **(1)**

      (ii) Suggest a reason for this relationship.

            _____

            _____ **(1)**

    (*c*) (i) With reference to **Figure 3**, calculate the total daily protein requirement of an eight-year-old and a seventy-year-old.

          Space for working

          Eight-year-old _____ Seventy-year-old _____ **(1)**

      (ii) Suggest an explanation for these figures.

            _____

            _____

            _____

            _____ **(2)**

Question 10 continues on page *eighteen*

Candidates must not write in this margin

Marks

10. (continued)

(*d*) (i) With reference to **Figures 2** and **3**, calculate the total bone mass of an average twenty-year-old person and an average seventy-year-old person.

Space for calculation

Twenty-year-old ____________ Seventy-year-old ____________ **(1)**

(ii) Calculate the average yearly loss of bone mass from the age of 20 to the age of 70.

Space for calculation

____________ g/year **(1)**

(iii) What information provided in **Figure 4** would suggest that it is misleading to calculate the average yearly loss of bone mass between the ages of 20 and 70?

____

____ **(1)**

(*e*) Osteoporosis is a condition in which bones tend to fracture more easily with age. What information from **Figures 2** and **4** can be used to explain this change?

____

____

____ **(1)**

Question 11 begins on page *nineteen*

11. The information in **Figures 1** to **3** relates to hypothermia, a condition which occurs when the body temperature falls below 35 °C.

Figure 1 Body dimensions of a ten-year-old child and a twenty-year-old man.

Individual	Mass (kg)	Height (cm)	Surface area (cm²)
Child	20	100	8000
Man	80	185	24 000

Figure 2 Body temperatures of a twenty-year-old man and a seventy-year-old man when exposed to an air temperature of 12 °C without thermal protection.

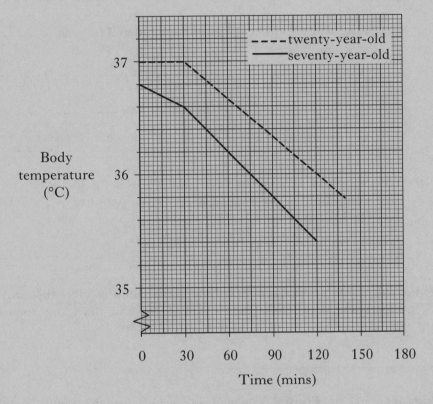

Figure 3 Number of hypothermia cases admitted to UK hospitals over a period of one year.

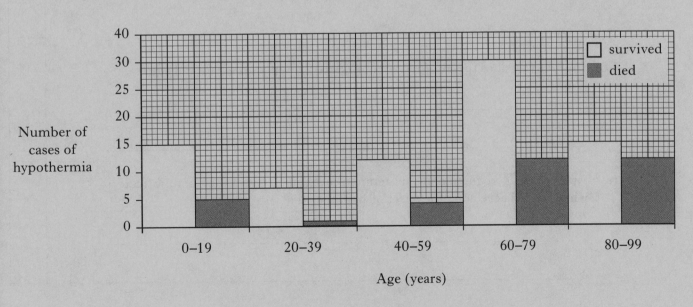

Question 11 continues on pages *twenty* and *twenty-one*

11. (continued)   *Marks*

(*a*)   (i)   Using the information from **Figure 1**, calculate the ratio of surface area
              to mass for the child and the man.

         Space for calculation

         Child _____ : _____   Man _____ : _____   **(1)**

        (ii)   Relate these figures to heat loss in the child and the man.

         _____

         _____

         _____   **(1)**

(*b*)   (i)   With reference to **Figure 2**, estimate how long the seventy-year-old
              man would need to be exposed to an air temperature of 12 °C before he
              develops hypothermia.

         _____   **(1)**

        (ii)   With reference to **Figure 2**, how many minutes after the start of the
              experiment does it take for the temperature of the young man to drop
              one degree?

         _____   **(1)**

(*c*)   With reference to **Figure 3**, which age group has the highest percentage
         survival rate from hypothermia?

         _____   **(1)**

(*d*)   In what way does the information in **Figure 2** support the data in **Figure 3**?

         _____

         _____   **(1)**

(*e*)   Apart from a reduction in air temperature, state **two** other abiotic factors
         which would accelerate the onset of hypothermia.

         1 _____

         2 _____   **(2)**

Question 11 continues on page *twenty-one*

Marks

11. **(continued)**

(f) Describe **one** voluntary and **one** involuntary response to a drop in body temperature below normal.

Voluntary response _____

_____

Involuntary response _____

_____ **(1)**

(g) Apart from low body temperature, state **two** symptoms of hypothermia.

1 _____

2 _____ **(1)**

[Turn over

12. Investigations can be carried out to determine the memory span for letters or numbers. *Marks*

(*a*) Given the lists of letters in **Table 1** below, describe how you would carry out an investigation to determine the human memory span for letters.

Table 1

LISTS OF LETTERS	D E G T
	S F B Y W
	L I W C Q R
	X B A Y I P W
	D M L Q T G H S
	F J I P W E R C B

_____

_____

_____

_____

_____

_____

_____

_____

_____

_____ **(3)**

Marks

12. (continued)

In another investigation to determine human memory span, a list of 70 sets of random numbers was used. One student was tested and the record kept of her performance is shown in the table below.

Table 2

| Length of List | Trial | | | | | | | | | | Percentage correct |
	1	2	3	4	5	6	7	8	9	10	--------------------
4 numbers	✓	✓	✓	✓	✓	✓	✓	✓	✓	✓	
5 numbers	✓	✓	✓	✓	✓	✓	✓	✓	✓	✓	
6 numbers	✓	✓	✓	✓	✓	✓	✓	✓	✓	✓	
7 numbers	✓	✓	✓	✓	✓	✓	✓	✓	✓	✓	
8 numbers	✓	✓	✗	✓	✓	✗	✗	✓	✗	✓	
9 numbers	✓	✗	✗	✗	✓	✗	✗	✗	✗	✓	
10 numbers	✗	✗	✗	✗	✗	✗	✗	✗	✗	✗	

✓ = correct response   ✗ = wrong response

(b) (i) Complete the last column of **Table 2** to show the percentage of responses which were correct.

(1)

(ii) Draw an appropriate bar graph to illustrate the results shown in **Table 2**.

(Additional graph paper, if required, will be found on page 26.)

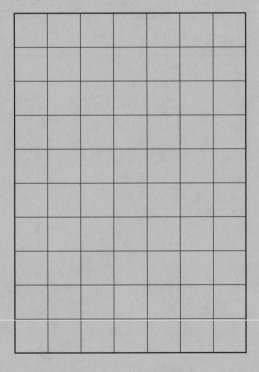

(2)

Marks

12. (continued)

(c) Describe a feature of this investigation which improves the reliability of the results obtained.

_____

_____

_____ **(1)**

(d) An independent observer scrutinised the results from this investigation and concluded that the human memory span was seven numbers.

Do you think this conclusion was valid? Give a reason for your answer.

Valid? _____

Reason for answer _____

_____

_____

_____ **(1)**

(e) Some students could improve their memory span by "chunking".
Describe what is meant by this term.

_____

_____

_____

_____ **(2)**

SECTION C

Answer BOTH questions 13 and 14 on the blank pages provided.

You may use labelled diagrams where appropriate.

Marks

13. Answer **either** A **or** B.

   A. Give an account of the impact of disease on the human population, under the following headings:

     (i) the regulatory effects of disease on populations;   **3**

     (ii) the use of vaccines to control major childhood diseases;   **7**

     (iii) the effects of improved hygiene and sanitation.   **5**

                                                            (15)

   OR

   B. Give an account of the different ways in which humans communicate, under the following headings:

     (i) the significance of communication to the human population;   **3**

     (ii) the use of language;   **5**

     (iii) non-verbal communication.   **7**

                                                            (15)

14. Answer **either** A **or** B.

   A. Describe the nitrogen cycle and indicate how it can be disrupted by the activities of human populations.   **(15)**

   OR

   B. Discuss the process and significance of cellular respiration.   **(15)**

[END OF QUESTION PAPER]

[Turn over

Marks

ADDITIONAL GRAPH PAPER FOR QUESTION 12(b).

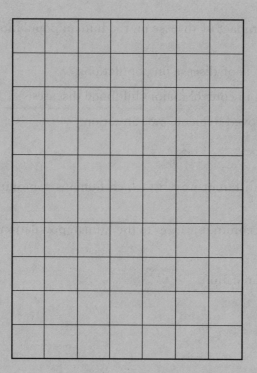

Marks

SPACE FOR ANSWERS

[Turn over

SPACE FOR ANSWERS

Marks

SPACE FOR ANSWERS

Marks

SPACE FOR ANSWERS

Candida
must n
write in
marg

FOR OFFICIAL USE

Presenting Centre No.	Subject No.	Level	Paper No.	Group No.	Marker's No.
	1800	**H**	**2**		

Total

1800/202

SCOTTISH
CERTIFICATE OF
EDUCATION
1999

WEDNESDAY, 12 MAY
9.00 AM – 11.30 AM

HUMAN BIOLOGY
HIGHER GRADE
Paper II

Fill in these boxes and read what is printed below.

Full name of school or college

Town

First name and initials

Surname

Date of birth
Day Month Year   Candidate number   Number of seat

1 (a)   All questions should be attempted.

   (b)   **Question 13 is on pages 18, 19 and 20 and Question 14 is on pages 21, 22 and 23—pages 20 and 21 are fold-out pages.**

   (c)   It should be noted that questions 15 and 16 each contain a choice.

2 The questions may be answered in any order but all answers are to be written in the spaces provided in this answer book, and must be written clearly and legibly in ink.

3 Additional space for answers and rough work will be found at the end of the book. If further space is required, supplementary sheets may be obtained from the invigilator and should be inserted inside the **front** cover of this booklet.

4 The numbers of questions must be clearly inserted with any answers written in the additional space.

5 Rough work, if any should be necessary, should be written in this booklet and then scored through when the fair copy has been written.

6 Before leaving the examination room you must give this book to the invigilator. If you do not, you may lose all the marks for this paper.

SCOTTISH
QUALIFICATIONS
AUTHORITY

SAB 1800/202 6/3/5470   ©

SECTION A

All questions in this section should be attempted.

Marks

1. The diagram below summarises different types of immunity.

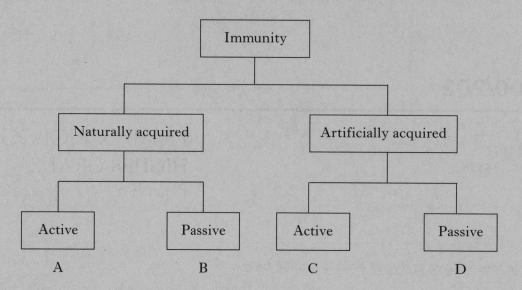

(a) Complete the table using the letters A, B, C and D to match correctly each type of immunity with its description.

Description of immunity	Letter
Ready-made antibodies are injected into the body.	
Babies get antibodies from breast milk.	
Bacteria enter the body and stimulate the production of antibodies.	
Foreign antigens are injected into the body and stimulate the production of antibodies.	

(2)

(b) The immune system sometimes over-reacts to a harmless substance.

What term is used to describe this reaction?

_____

(1)

Candidates must not write in this margin

Marks

1. (continued)

(*c*) Rheumatoid arthritis is a condition in which the body attacks its own cells. What term is used to describe this type of condition?

______________________________ **(1)**

(*d*) After kidney transplant surgery, drugs are taken by the patient to reduce the normal immune response. Explain why this drug treatment is necessary.

____

____

____

______________________________ **(2)**

[Turn over

Marks

2. The diagram below shows an enzyme-catalysed reaction taking place in the presence of an inhibitor.

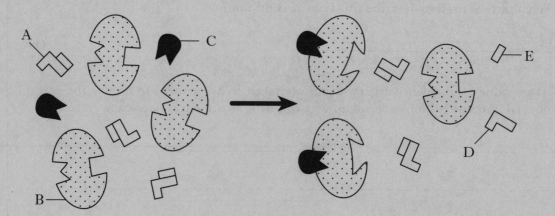

(a) Using **all** the letters from the diagram, complete the table below.

Molecules in reaction	Letter(s)
Enzyme	
Substrate	
Products	
Inhibitor	

(2)

(b) Explain how this inhibitor works.

_____

_____

_____

_____   (2)

Marks

2. **(continued)**

(*c*) State the effect of increasing substrate concentration on the rate of enzyme activity and give an explanation for your answer.

Effect _____

Explanation _____

_____

_____

_____ **(2)**

(*d*) The diagram below shows a metabolic pathway.

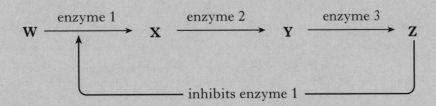

    (i) Explain how the concentration of Z is controlled.

    _____

    _____

    _____ **(1)**

    (ii) Explain the benefit of this type of control system to the body.

    _____

    _____ **(1)**

(*e*) The pancreas produces an enzyme which digests protein. Explain why a sample of juice taken directly from the pancreas would not break down protein.

_____

_____ **(1)**

[Turn over

Candida
must n
write in
margi

3. The diagram below shows two pairs of chromosomes from a cell undergoing *Marks* meiosis.

PAIR 1   PAIR 2

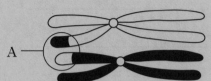   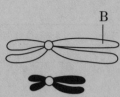

(a) Is this cell undergoing the first or second meiotic division?
Give a reason for your answer.

Division _____

Reason _____

_____ **(1)**

(b) Where in the body would this cell be found?

_____ **(1)**

(c) Name structure B.

_____ **(1)**

(d) (i) What process has occurred in area A?

_____ **(1)**

(ii) Explain the significance of this process in gamete production.

_____

_____ **(1)**

(e) In the diagram above, which pair of chromosomes are autosomes?
Give a reason for your answer.

Pair _____

Reason _____ **(1)**

Candidates must not write in this margin

Marks

4. Three different alleles determine the ABO blood groups. Allele *A* and allele *B* are both dominant to allele *O*.

(*a*) Alleles *A* and *B* are both expressed in heterozygous individuals who have blood group AB. What term is used to describe the relationship between alleles *A* and *B*?

______________________________ **(1)**

(*b*) (i) A man with blood group AB marries a woman with blood group O. State the genotypes of the parental gametes and use them to complete the Punnett diagram below.

	man		woman
parental phenotypes	AB	×	O
gamete genotypes	____ ____		____ ____

(1)

Punnett diagram

male gametes / female gametes		

(1)

(ii) State the possible phenotypes of the children and the ratio in which they would be expected to occur.

Phenotypes ______________________________

Ratio ______________________________ **(1)**

(iii) Which of the parents would be able to donate blood safely to any of their children? Give a reason for your answer.

Parent ______________________________

Reason ____

____ **(1)**

[Turn over

5. The diagram below shows how hormones from the pituitary gland affect the *Marks* ovary.

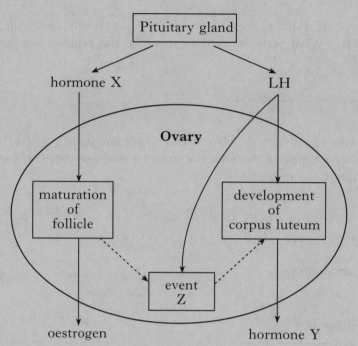

(*a*) Name hormones X and Y.

X _____

Y _____ **(1)**

(*b*) What term is used to describe event Z?

_____ **(1)**

(*c*) Describe **one** effect of oestrogen on

(i) the pituitary gland; _____

_____ **(1)**

(ii) the uterus. _____

_____ **(1)**

(*d*) In what way do the chemicals in the contraceptive pill affect hormone production by the pituitary gland?

_____

_____ **(1)**

Candidates
must not
write in this
margin

6. The diagram below shows the liver with its associated organs and blood vessels.

Marks

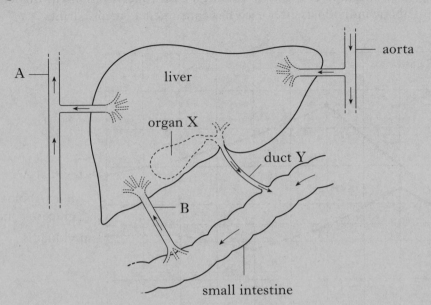

(a) Name blood vessels A and B.

A _____

B _____   **(2)**

(b) Complete the table below to show how the concentrations of glucose and urea in the blood change as the blood flows from B to A through the liver.

	After a heavy meal	*During a period of starvation*
glucose		
urea	increase	

(2)

(c) (i) Name organ X.

_____   **(1)**

(ii) Name the chemical compound, present in the liquid in duct Y, which is formed from the breakdown of haemoglobin.

_____   **(1)**

(iii) Describe **one** function of the liquid carried in duct Y.

_____   **(1)**

Marks

7. (*a*) The graph below shows changes in blood glucose concentrations in diabetic and non-diabetic individuals after each has consumed a glucose drink.

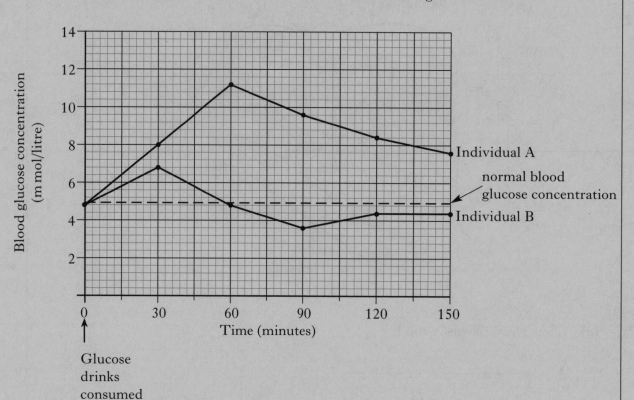

(i) Which individual is diabetic? Give **two** reasons for your answer.

Diabetic _____

Reason 1 _____

_____

Reason 2 _____

_____ **(2)**

(ii) Explain why the blood glucose concentration of individual A starts to drop after one hour.

_____

_____

_____ **(1)**

Marks

7. (continued)

(b) The diagram below summarises the body's blood glucose regulating mechanism.

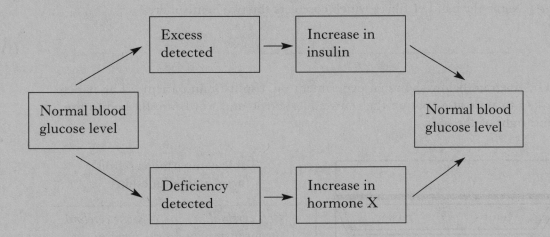

(i) Name hormone X and state where it is produced.

Hormone X _____   **(1)**

Site of production _____   **(1)**

(ii) Glucose is stored as an insoluble carbohydrate. Name this carbohydrate and explain why it is important that it is insoluble.

Carbohydrate _____   **(1)**

Explanation _____

_____

_____   **(1)**

[Turn over

8. Split-brain patients cannot transfer information between their left and right cerebral hemispheres because the nerve fibres connecting these areas of the brain have been cut.

(a) Name the band of fibres which connects the two hemispheres.

_____

(1)

The diagram below shows an experiment on a split-brain patient. The patient is asked to stare at a spot on the centre of a screen and words are flashed to the left and right of the spot.

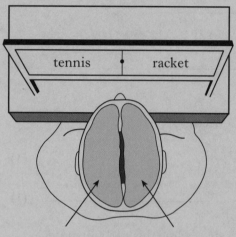

tennis · racket

left cerebral
hemisphere

right cerebral
hemisphere

Table comparing cerebral
hemisphere functions

Left cerebral hemisphere	*Right cerebral hemisphere*
processes information from right eye	processes information from left eye
controls language production	controls spatial task coordination

(b) The words "tennis" and "racket" are flashed briefly onto the screen as shown. Use the information in the table to explain why the patient states that he has seen the word racket but that he cannot say what kind of racket it is.

_____

_____

_____

(2)

8 (a) Corpus

(b) he cannot say which type of racket it is because the LCH is receiving information from the right eye and the LCH controls language he therefore can say racket. But the RCH is responsible for spacial task coordination and processes info from the left eye.

Marks

9. The diagram below shows the processes which link short-term memory and long-term memory.

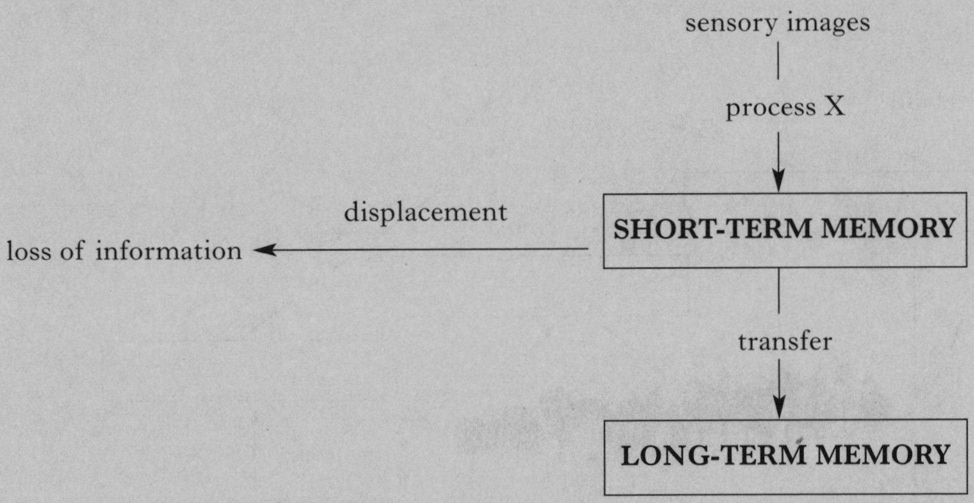

sensory images

|

process X

↓

displacement

loss of information ◄─────────────── **SHORT-TERM MEMORY**

transfer

↓

LONG-TERM MEMORY

(a) Name process X.

_____ **(1)**

(b) Explain why some of the information in short-term memory is displaced.

_____ **(1)**

(c) Describe **one** method of transferring information from short-term memory to long-term memory.

_____

_____ **(1)**

(d) (i) Name **one** area of the brain thought to be involved in memory storage.

_____ **(1)**

(ii) Name a neurotransmitter involved in the formation of memories.

_____ **(1)**

[Turn over

10. The diagram below shows the water cycle.

Marks

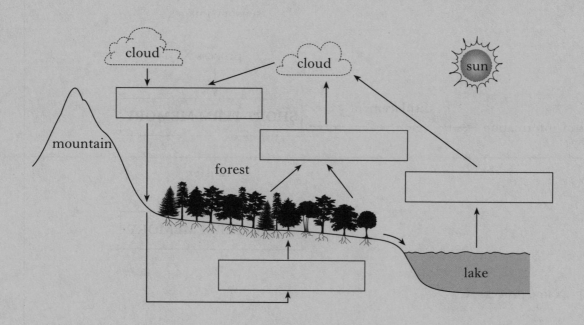

(a) Use **all** the words from the list below to complete the diagram above.

evaporation	precipitation	transpiration	absorption

(1)

(b) What term is used to describe the large-scale removal of trees?

_____

(1)

(c) Describe **two** effects on the water cycle of large-scale removal of trees.

1 _____

_____

2 _____

_____

(1)

(d) Apart from its effect on the water cycle, describe **two** other consequences of the large-scale removal of trees.

1 _____

_____

2 _____

_____

(1)

Marks

11. The graph below shows the populations of algae and bacteria at various points along a river into which untreated sewage is flowing.

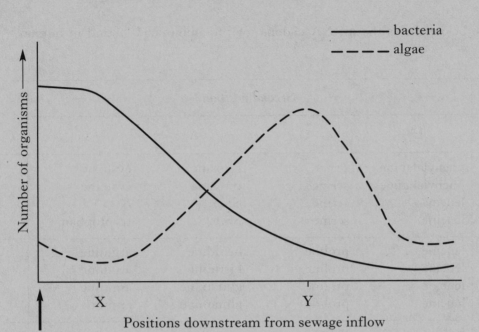

(*a*) Explain the change in the population of bacteria between points X and Y in the river.

_____

_____

_____ **(1)**

(*b*) Explain the change in the population of algae between points X and Y in the river.

_____

_____

_____ **(1)**

(*c*) What term is used to describe the large population of algae at point Y?

_____ **(1)**

[Turn over

SECTION B

All questions in this section should be attempted.

12. The table below shows the mRNA codons for the amino acids found in human protein.

First position	Second position				Third position
	U	C	A	G	
U	phenylalanine phenylalanine leucine leucine	serine serine serine serine	tyrosine tyrosine *Stop* *Stop*	cysteine cysteine *Stop* tryptophan	U C A G
C	leucine leucine leucine leucine	proline proline proline proline	histidine histidine glutamine glutamine	arginine arginine arginine arginine	U C A G
A	isoleucine isoleucine isoleucine methionine/*Start*	threonine threonine threonine threonine	asparagine asparagine lysine lysine	serine serine arginine arginine	U C A G
G	valine valine valine valine	alanine alanine alanine alanine	aspartic acid aspartic acid glutamic acid glutamic acid	glycine glycine glycine glycine	U C A G

Marks

(a) (i) From the table, the mRNA codon for tryptophan is U (first position) G (second position) G (third position). What are the **two** mRNA codons for the amino acid asparagine?

_____   and _____   **(1)**

(ii) How many mRNA codons are there for the amino acid serine?

_____   **(1)**

(iii) State the tRNA anti-codon for the amino acid tryptophan.

_____   **(1)**

Marks

12.   (continued)

(*b*)   How many different triplet codons are there?

_____   **(1)**

(*c*)   The diagram below shows the base sequence in part of a DNA strand.

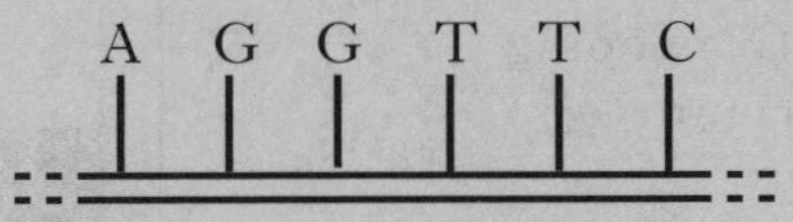

A   G   G   T   T   C

(i)   What two amino acids are coded for by this strand of DNA?

_____ and _____   **(1)**

(ii)   If the base A was replaced by the base C as a result of a mutation in the strand above, which two amino acids would result?

_____ and _____   **(1)**

(iii)   What name is given to this type of mutation?

_____   **(1)**

(iv)   Why is this type of mutation potentially less harmful than an insertion or deletion mutation?

_____

_____

_____

_____ **(2)**

(*d*)   Name bases A and C.

A _____   _____ C _____ **(1)**

[Turn over

13. The figures below give information about different aspects of the human population worldwide. The population of the world in 1999 is six thousand million (6×10^9).

Figure 1 Distribution of world population

Figure 2 Distribution of medical provision

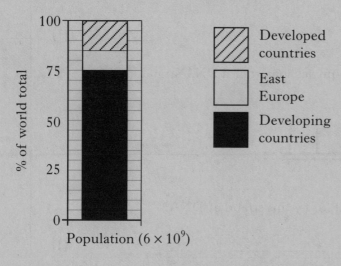

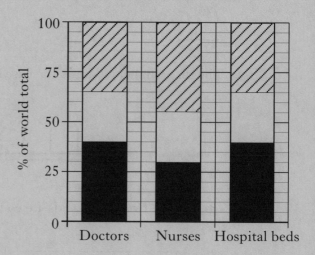

Figure 3 World birth and death rates

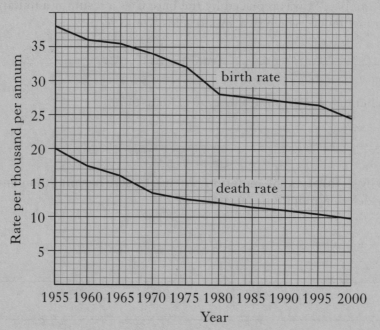

Figure 4 Population structure and fertility rates in 1999

Area	% of population in each age range			Fertility rate (average number of children/woman)
	0–15 (years)	15–64 (years)	64+ (years)	
Developed countries	19·5	66·5	14·0	1·8
East Europe	23·0	65·7	11·3	2·3
Developing countries	42·3	54·1	3·6	6·5

Question 13 continues on pages *nineteen* and fold out page *twenty*

Marks

13.   (continued)

(*a*)   (i)   Calculate the total population of the developing countries.

Space for calculation

_____ million   **(1)**

(ii)   With reference to **Figure 1** and **Figure 2**, which part of the world has the highest proportion of doctors **per head of population**?

_____   **(1)**

(*b*)   Describe **one** trend shown by the graphs in **Figure 3** and suggest an explanation for this trend.

Trend _____

Explanation _____

_____   **(1)**

(*c*)   (i)   With reference to **Figure 3**, state the world birth rates and death rates in 1999.

Birth date _____

Death rate _____   **(1)**

(ii)   With reference to **Figure 1** and the answer given in (*c*)(i), calculate the expected increase in the population of the world this year.

Space for calculation

_____ million   **(1)**

(*d*)   What **two** factors, other than birth rate and death rate, should be considered when calculating changes in populations of different countries?

_____ and _____   **(1)**

Question 13 continues on page *twenty*

13. (continued)

Marks

(e) Which area of the world shown in **Figure 4** has the greatest potential for population growth? Give **two** reasons for your answer.

Area _____ **(1)**

Reason 1 _____

_____

Reason 2 _____

_____ **(1)**

(f) Infant mortality is high in developing countries. With reference to the data in **Figures 1**, **2** and **4**, suggest **two** possible explanations for this.

Explanation 1 _____

_____

_____ **(1)**

Explanation 2 _____

_____

_____ **(1)**

Question 14 begins on page *twenty-one*

Marks

14. (a) Complete **Table 1** below to show the structure and class of a number of carbohydrates.

Table 1

Carbohydrate	Simplified structure	Class
glucose	⬭	monosaccharide
fructose	⬭	
sucrose	⬭—⬭	
maltose		disaccharide
starch		

(2)

(b) A number of reagents are used to test for different carbohydrates.
Table 2 below describes four positive test results using these reagents.

Table 2

A	Colour change from purple to red	B	Colour change from blue to orange
C	Colour change from brown to blue-black	D	Colour change from pink to purple

(i) Complete **Table 3** below using any of the letters A to D to match each reagent with a positive test result.

Table 3

Reagent	Positive test result
Iodine solution	
Clinistix strip	
Benedict's solution	

(2)

Question 14 continues on pages *twenty-two* and *twenty-three*

14. **(*b*)** **(continued)**   *Marks*

(ii) What procedure must be carried out when using Benedict's solution and Barfoed's reagent, but should not be carried out when using Clinistix or Iodine solution?

_____

(1)

(*c*) **Table 4** below shows results which were obtained when testing various carbohydrates.

Table 4

Carbohydrate	Test				
	Solubility	*Barfoed's*	*Benedict's*	*Iodine*	*Clinistix*
glucose	+	+	+	−	+
starch	−	−	−	+	−
sucrose	+	−	−	−	−
maltose	+	−	+	−	−
fructose	+	+	+	−	−

+   positive result
−   negative result

(i) Which test could be used to distinguish maltose from sucrose?

_____

(1)

Question 14 continues on page *twenty-three*

Marks

14. **(c)** **(continued)**

(ii) Using the information in **Table 4**, construct a branching identification key showing the tests you would use to identify the carbohydrates in the table.

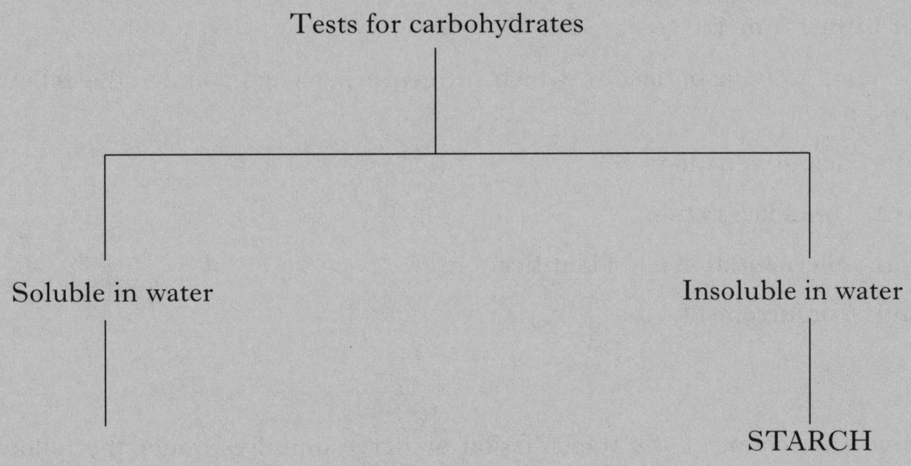

Tests for carbohydrates

Soluble in water   Insoluble in water

STARCH

(2)

(d) When sucrose is heated with acid for a few minutes then neutralised with alkali, it gives a positive test with Benedict's solution. Suggest an explanation for this.

_____

_____

_____ (2)

Marks

SECTION C

Answer BOTH questions 15 and 16 on the blank pages provided.

You may use labelled diagrams where appropriate.

15. Answer **either** A **or** B.

    A. Give an account of factors which influence behaviour, under the following headings:

        (i)   deindividuation;   **4**

        (ii)   social facilitation;   **4**

        (iii)   internalisation and identification;   **4**

        (iv)   reinforcement.   **3**

        (15)

OR

    B. Give an account of the transmission of nerve impulses under the following headings:

        (i)   the structure of neurones;   **4**

        (ii)   the synapse;   **7**

        (iii)   converging pathways;   **2**

        (iv)   diverging pathways.   **2**

        (15)

16. Answer **either** A **or** B.

    A. Describe how heart rate is controlled.   **(15)**

OR

    B. Describe ways in which humans have overcome the problems of food supply since the beginning of agricultural practices.   **(15)**

[END OF QUESTION PAPER]

SPACE FOR ANSWERS

Marks

[Turn over

SPACE FOR ANSWERS

Marks

SPACE FOR ANSWERS

Marks

Page twenty–seven

[Turn over

SPACE FOR ANSWERS

Marks

[BLANK PAGE]

[BLANK PAGE]

FOR OFFICIAL USE

Presenting Centre No.	Subject No.	Level	Paper No.	Group No.	Marker's No.

Total ☐

[C009/SQP023]

Higher   Time: 2 hours 30 minutes   **NATIONAL**
Human Biology   **QUALIFICATIONS**
Specimen Question Paper

Fill in these boxes and read what is printed below.

Full name of school or college

Town

First name and initials

Surname

Date of birth
Day Month Year   Candidate number   Number of seat

SECTION A—Questions 1–30
Instructions for completion of Section A are given on page two.

SECTIONS B AND C

1   (a)   All questions should be attempted.

     (b)   It should be noted that in **Section C** questions 1 and 2 each contain a choice.

2   The questions may be answered in any order but all answers are to be written in the spaces provided in this answer book, and must be written clearly and legibly in ink.

3   Additional space for answers and rough work will be found at the end of the book. If further space is required, supplementary sheets may be obtained from the invigilator and should be inserted inside the **front** cover of this book.

4   The numbers of questions must be clearly inserted with any answers written in the additional space.

5   Rough work, if any should be necessary, should be written in this book and then scored through when the fair copy has been written.

6   Before leaving the examination room you must give this book to the invigilator. If you do not, you may lose all the marks for this paper.

SCOTTISH
QUALIFICATIONS
AUTHORITY
©

SECTION A

Read carefully

1   Check that the answer sheet provided is for Higher Human Biology (Section A).

2   Fill in the details required on the answer sheet.

3   In this section a question is answered by indicating the choice A, B, C or D by a stroke made in **ink** in the appropriate place in the answer sheet—see the sample question below.

4   For each question there is only **one** correct answer.

5   Rough working, if required, should be done only on this question paper—or on the rough working sheet provided—**not** on the answer sheet.

6   At the end of the examination the answer sheet for Section A **must not** be placed inside this answer book, but should be handed separately to the invigilator.

Sample Question

The digestive enzyme pepsin is most active in the

A   mouth

B   stomach

C   duodenum

D   pancreas.

The correct answer is **B**—stomach. A **heavy** vertical line should be drawn joining the two dots in the appropriate box in the column headed **B** as shown in the example on the answer sheet.

If, after you have recorded your answer, you decide that you have made an error and wish to make a change, you should cancel the original answer and put a vertical stroke in the box you now consider to be correct. Thus, if you want to change an answer D to an answer B, your answer sheet would look like this:

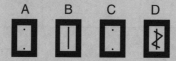

If you want to change back to an answer which has already been scored out, you should enter a tick (✓) to the **right** of the box of your choice, thus:

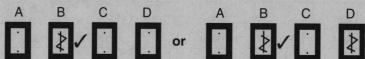

SECTION A

All questions in this section should be attempted.

Answers should be given on the separate answer sheet provided.

1. Which of the following substances are both polysaccharides?

   A   Glycogen and glucose

   B   Starch and maltose

   C   Maltose and glucose

   D   Glycogen and starch

2. Which of the following substances does **not** contain the element nitrogen?

   A   Protein

   B   Pepsin

   C   Ammonia

   D   Glycogen

3. Which of the following is a function of lipid molecules?

   A   They act as antibodies.

   B   They transport vitamins.

   C   They assist muscular contractions.

   D   They act as biological catalysts.

4. When a protease enzyme is added to an amylase solution, which of the following could be produced?

   A   Amino acids

   B   Maltose

   C   Glucose

   D   Glycerol

5. The mRNA codon for the amino acid tyrosine is UAU. Which of the following base sequences is the tRNA anticodon for tyrosine?

   A   TUT

   B   ATA

   C   GTG

   D   AUA

6. A section of a DNA molecule contains 80 bases. Of these, 24 are thymine.

   The percentage of cytosine bases in the molecule is

   A   12%

   B   16%

   C   20%

   D   32%.

7. The diagram below represents stages in tissue respiration.

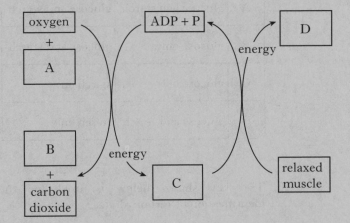

   Which box represents glucose?

8. Which of the following substances are produced during the Krebs cycle?

   A   Carbon dioxide and hydrogen

   B   Carbon dioxide and water

   C   ATP and oxygen

   D   ATP and water

Page three

9. The following experiment was set up and left for 24 hours.

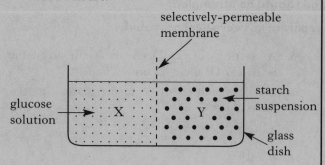

Which carbohydrates would be present in X and Y after the 24 hours?

	X	Y
A	glucose and starch	glucose and starch
B	glucose only	glucose and starch
C	glucose only	starch only
D	glucose and starch	starch only

10. The key shown below is used for the identification of carbohydrates.

1	soluble	2
	insoluble	Glycogen
2	Benedict's text positive	3
	Benedict's test negative	Sucrose
3	Barfoed's test positive	4
	Barfoed's test negative	Lactose
4	Clinistix test positive	Glucose
	Clinistix test negative	Fructose

Which line in the table of results below is **not** in agreement with the information contained in the key?

	Carbohydrate	Benedict's test	Barfoed's test	Clinistix test
A	Lactose	positive	negative	not tested
B	Glucose	positive	negative	positive
C	Fructose	positive	positive	negative
D	Sucrose	negative	not tested	not tested

11. A student requires $100 \, cm^3$ of urea solution of strength $0 \cdot 25 \, M$. How may this solution be obtained from a $0 \cdot 5 \, M$ stock solution?

A By adding $50 \, cm^3$ of water to $50 \, cm^3$ of stock solution

B By adding $33 \cdot 3 \, cm^3$ of stock solution to $66 \cdot 6 \, cm^3$ of water

C By concentrating the stock solution five times

D By diluting the stock solution five times

12. Viruses are composed principally of

A protein and lipid

B nucleic acid and protein

C lipid and carbohydrate

D nucleic acid and carbohydrate.

13. A person exposed to a disease-causing antigen may suffer from that disease.

This person may then be immune to the disease.

This is an example of

A artificial active immunity

B natural active immunity

C artificial passive immunity

D natural passive immunity.

14. A person has blood group O.

Which entry on the table identifies correctly the antigens and antibodies present?

	Antigens on cells	Antibodies in plasma
A	A and B	Anti-a and Anti-b
B	None	Anti-a and Anti-b
C	A and B	None
D	None	None

15. Red-green colour-blindness is a sex-linked recessive trait. A woman whose father is colour-blind marries a man with normal vision. If they have a son, what are the chances that he will be colour-blind?

    A   0%

    B   25%

    C   50%

    D   100%

16. Oxytocin is released by the

    A   ovaries

    B   placenta

    C   corpus luteum

    D   pituitary.

17. Monozygotic twins result from

    A   one fertilised egg cell

    B   one egg cell and two sperm

    C   two egg cells and one sperm

    D   two egg cells and two sperm.

18. The following data refer to the breathing of an athlete (a) resting and (b) just after a race.

	Breathing rate (per minute)	Volume of one breath	% Carbon dioxide in exhaled air
Resting (a)	10	300 ml	5
After race (b)	20	1 litre	5

    Assuming the rate of breathing remains constant, what would be the volume of carbon dioxide breathed out during the ten minutes after the race?

    A   500 ml

    B   1000 ml

    C   5 litres

    D   10 litres

19. The diagram below is of a heart.

    Which label identifies the position of the sinoatrial node (SAN)?

    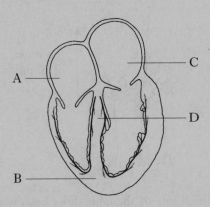

20. The durations of diastole and systole are shown below.

    Diastole   0·3 seconds
    Systole   0·1 seconds

    What is the heart rate of this individual?

    A   48 beats per minute

    B   75 beats per minute

    C   150 beats per minute

    D   240 beats per minute

Questions 21 and 22 refer to the drawing of a section through the brain.

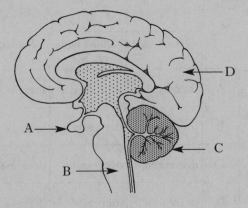

21. Which letter indicates the part of the brain which controls heart rate?

22. Which letter indicates the cerebral cortex?

23. The following diagram represents four neurones in a nervous pathway.

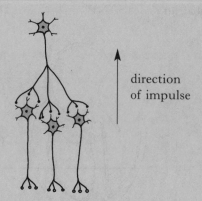

direction of impulse

Which line of the table describes the pathway correctly?

		Type of pathway
A	motor	divergent
B	motor	convergent
C	sensory	divergent
D	sensory	convergent

24. Which line of the table shows correctly the influence of the parasympathetic nervous system?

	Heartbeat	Blood flow to gut	Sweating
A	increased	increased	increased
B	increased	decreased	increased
C	decreased	decreased	decreased
D	decreased	increased	decreased

25. The average span of the short-term memory is

A   less than 4 items

B   around 7 items

C   around 10 items

D   more than 12 items.

26. Which procedure would allow the change in size of a human population to be calculated?

A   Adding births to deaths and subtracting immigrations and emigrations

B   Adding births to emigrations and subtracting deaths and immigrations

C   Adding births to immigrations and subtracting deaths and emigrations

D   Adding deaths to immigrations and subtracting births and emigrations

27. The table shows the birth rates and death rates in four continents.

Continents	Birth rate per 1000	Death rate per 1000
Africa	46	20
North America	18	9
South America	39	10
Europe	18	10

Which line of the table below identifies correctly the continents with the highest and lowest population growth rates?

	POPULATION GROWTH RATES	
	Highest	Lowest
A	Africa	North America
B	Africa	Europe
C	South America	North America
D	South America	Europe

28. The population pyramid for a country is shown below.

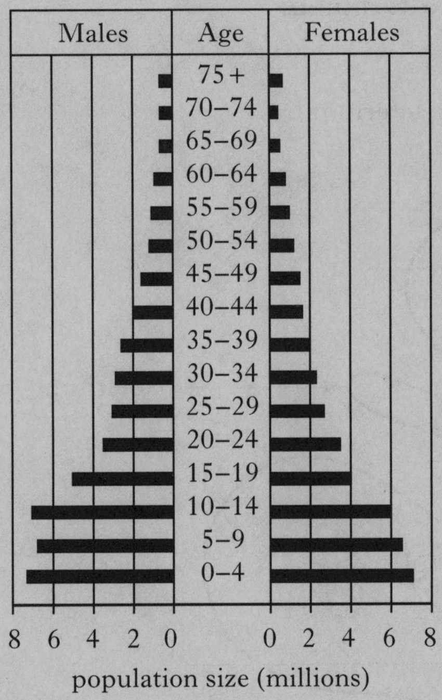

Males	Age	Females
	75+	
	70-74	
	65-69	
	60-64	
	55-59	
	50-54	
	45-49	
	40-44	
	35-39	
	30-34	
	25-29	
	20-24	
	15-19	
	10-14	
	5-9	
	0-4	

8 6 4 2 0   0 2 4 6 8
population size (millions)

How many males are there between the ages of 10 and 19?

A   6 million

B   7 million

C   12 million

D   22 million

29. Algal blooms in lakes are most likely to be the result of

A   low oxygen concentrations

B   over-fishing

C   fertiliser run-off

D   nitrogen deficiency.

30. Which of the following processes keeps atmospheric carbon dioxide concentrations low?

A   Decomposition

B   Nitrogen fixation

C   Respiration

D   Photosynthesis

Candidates are reminded that the answer sheet MUST NOT be returned <u>inside</u> this answer book.

Marks

SECTION B

All questions in this section should be attempted.

1. The diagram below shows a macrophage engulfing a bacterium.

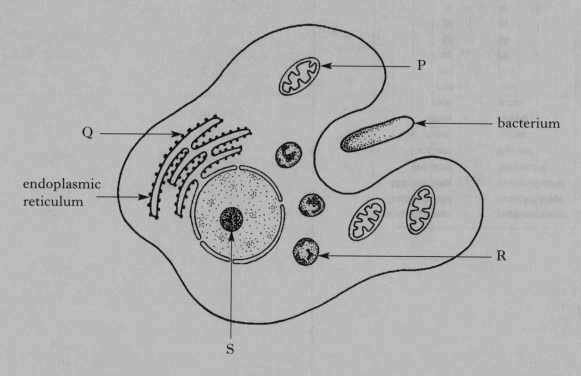

(a) The table gives some information about organelles shown in the diagram. Complete the table by inserting the appropriate letters, names and functions.

Letter	Name of organelle	Function
P		provides ATP for membrane movement
	Lysosome	
		synthesis of protein

(3)

(b) What term is used to describe the engulfing process shown in the diagram?

_____

(1)

Candidates must not write in this margin

Marks

1. (continued)

(*c*) Another type of white blood cell could destroy this bacterium by producing antibodies.

(i) Name this type of white blood cell.

______________________________ **(1)**

(ii) What feature of the bacterium stimulates the production of antibodies?

______________________________ **(1)**

(iii) Describe how the production of antibodies can be stimulated artificially.

____

____ **(1)**

2.   The diagram below shows part of a nucleic acid molecule.   *Marks*

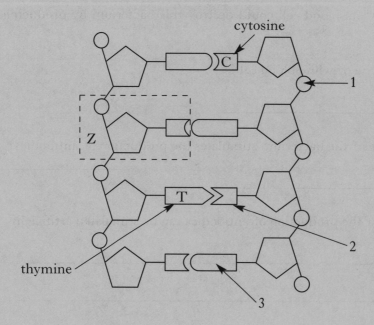

(a)   (i)   Which type of nucleic acid is shown in the diagram?

_____   **(1)**

(ii)   Name the part of the molecule inside box Z.

_____   **(1)**

(iii)   Identify parts labelled 1, 2 and 3 on the diagram.

1 _____

2 _____

3 _____   **(2)**

(b)   Describe a structural feature of this nucleic acid not shown in the diagram
      above.

_____   **(1)**

(c)   During replication of a nucleic acid the base sequence might be copied
      incorrectly.

(i)   Give the term used to describe this type of alteration.

_____   **(1)**

(ii)   Describe how this alteration might affect a metabolic pathway.

_____

_____   **(1)**

Marks

3. The family tree below shows the inheritance of a genetic disorder.

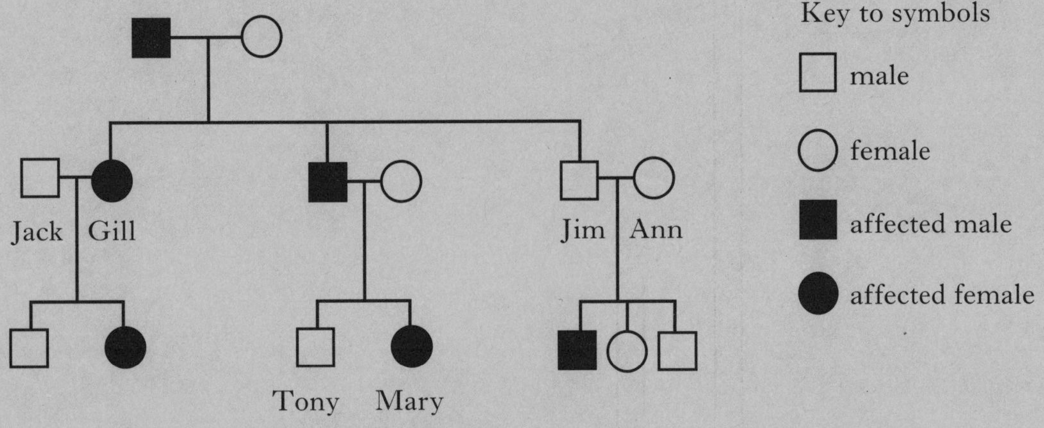

Key to symbols

☐ male

○ female

■ affected male

● affected female

(a) State whether the disorder is dominant or recessive and give a reason for your answer.

Dominant/recessive _____   **(1)**

Reason _____

_____

_____   **(1)**

(b) Using symbols **B** and **b** to represent the alleles, give the genotypes of Tony and Mary.

Tony _____   Mary _____   **(1)**

(c) Jack and Gill are expecting a third child.
What is the percentage chance of this child inheriting the disorder?

_____ %   **(1)**

4. The diagram below represents the two sex chromosomes.

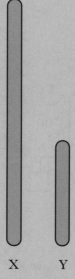

X   Y

(*a*) Using the letter H, mark on the diagram the likely position of the sex-linked allele which causes haemophilia.

(1)

(*b*) What term is used to describe the other 44 chromosomes found in a normal diploid cell?

_____

(1)

(*c*) Describe how a karyotype can be used to detect genetic disorders.

_____

_____

(1)

Marks

5.   The diagrams below show a sperm and an ovum.

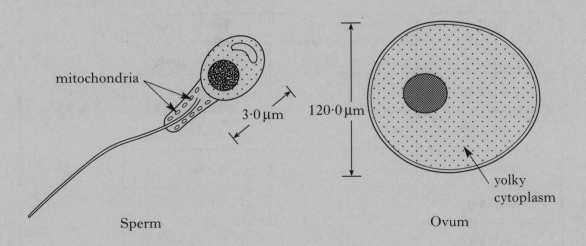

Sperm   Ovum

(*a*)   (i)   Calculate the total length of the sperm.

_____   **(1)**

(ii)   Express the length of the sperm and the length of the ovum as a simple ratio.

_____ : _____   **(1)**
sperm   ovum

(iii)   Explain why there is such a difference in size between the ovum and the sperm.

_____

_____   **(1)**

(*b*)   Why is it necessary for sperm to have large numbers of mitochondria?

_____

_____   **(1)**

(*c*)   Complete the table below to show the functions of FSH and LH (ICSH) in males.

Hormone	Function
FSH	
LH (ICSH)	

(2)

Page thirteen

6. The table below shows the results of an investigation into the relationship between the birth weight of babies and concentrations of lead and zinc in the placentas.

Birth weight (kg)	Average lead concentration in placenta ($\mu g/kg$)	Average zinc concentration in placenta ($\mu g/kg$)
2·00–2·49	31	33
2·50–2·99	22	41
3·00–3·49	13	60
3·50–3·99	12	58
4·00–4·49	11	55
4·50–4·99	13	59

(a) Present the data in a suitable form on the graph paper.

(Additional graph paper, if required, will be found on page 16.)

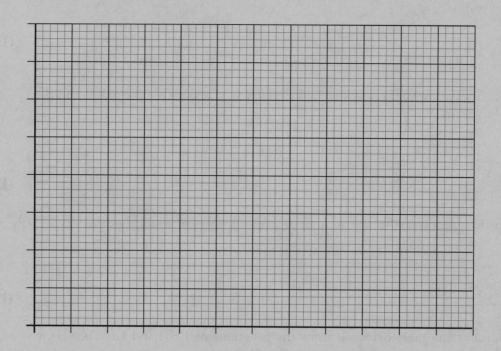

(3)

Candidates must not write in this margin

Marks

6. (continued)

(*b*) (i) Describe the relationship between placental lead and birth weight and between placental zinc and birth weight.

Lead ______________________________

____

Zinc ______________________________

______________________________ **(2)**

(ii) Suggest the effect of zinc on enzyme activity.

______________________________ **(1)**

(*c*) How might a metal ion, such as lead, reach the placenta from the environment?

____

____

______________________________ **(2)**

ADDITIONAL GRAPH PAPER FOR QUESTION 6

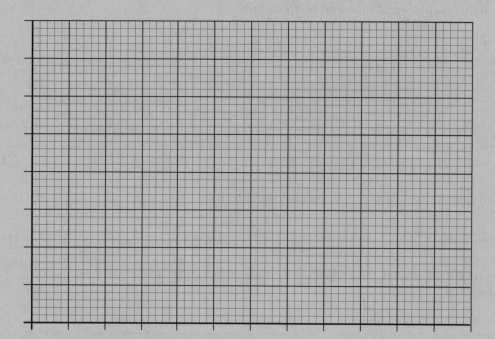

7. The diagram below shows the relationship between the ovarian hormones A and B *Marks*
and the thickness of the endometrium of the uterus.

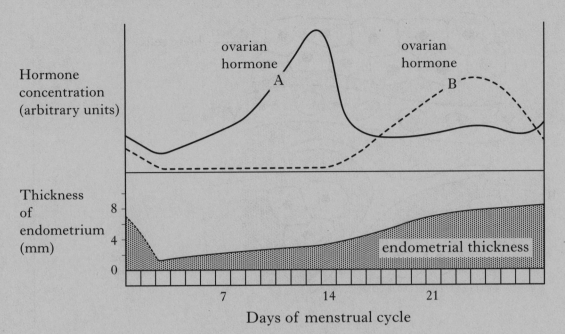

Days of menstrual cycle

(a) Name the hormones A and B.

A _____

B _____   **(2)**

(b) Shade in **five** boxes under the graph which correspond to the fertile period.   **(1)**

(c) Describe **two** events which occur in the Graafian follicle during the fertile
period.

1 _____

_____

2 _____

_____   **(2)**

(d) (i) What is the function of the endometrium?

_____   **(1)**

(ii) What happens to the endometrium if a woman becomes pregnant?

_____   **(1)**

8. The diagram below shows the relationship between the circulatory system and body cells.

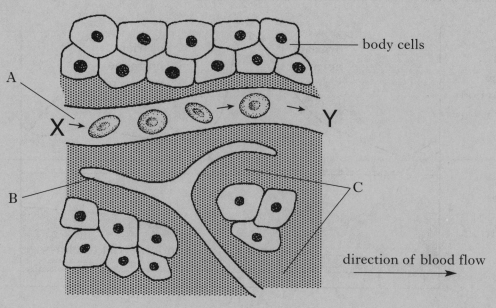

(a) Identify fluids found at A, B and C.

A _____

B _____

C _____ **(2)**

(b) The composition of blood changes as it flows between points X and Y on the diagram. Complete the table below using the words **increase** or **decrease** to indicate the changes which occur.

Substance	Change in concentration X→Y
Glucose	
Oxygen	
Carbon dioxide	
Metabolic waste	

(1)

(c) Explain why the blood pressure drops as the blood flows from point X to point Y.

_____

_____ **(1)**

Marks

9. The graph below shows changes in the body temperature of a student during an experiment in which she puts her arm into hot water.

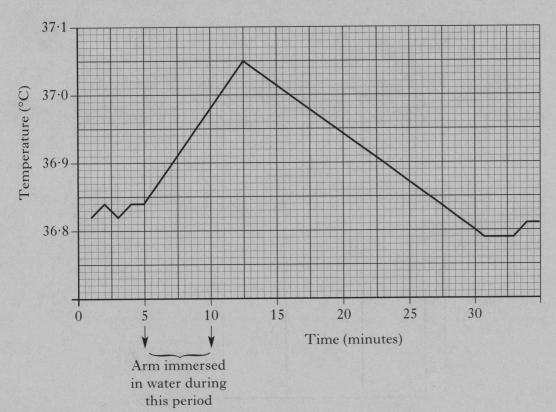

Arm immersed
in water during
this period

(*a*)   (i)   What was the highest temperature recorded?

_____

(1)

(ii)   Explain why the body temperature increased when the arm was placed in the hot water.

_____

_____

(1)

(iii) Suggest a reason why the body temperature was lower at the end of the experiment than at the beginning.

_____

_____

(1)

(*b*)   (i)   Where in the brain is body temperature monitored?

_____

(1)

(ii)   Which division of the nervous system is involved in the involuntary control of body temperature?

_____

(1)

10. The three Figures below show data relating to the ageing process.

Figure 1

Changes in body tissue composition with age

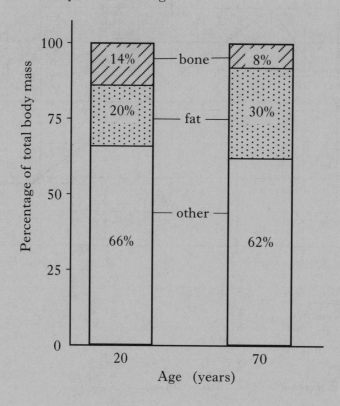

Figure 2

Changes in protein requirement with age

Age (years)	Average daily protein required (g/kg body mass)	Average body mass (kg)
8	1·5	28
20	0·8	75
70	0·6	70

Figure 3

Changes in bone density with age

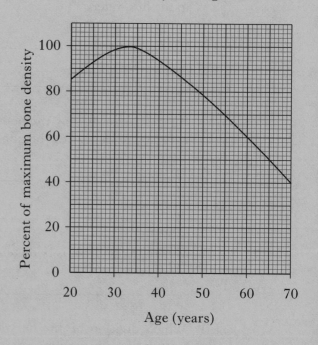

Candidates must not write in this margin

Marks

10. (continued)

(*a*) With reference to **Figures 1** and **2**, calculate the total bone mass of an average twenty-year-old person and an average seventy-year-old person.

Space for calculation

Twenty-year-old ______________ Seventy-year-old ______________ **(1)**

(*b*) Calculate the average yearly loss of bone mass from the age of 20 to the age of 70.

Space for calculation

______________ g/year **(1)**

(*c*) What information provided in **Figure 3** would suggest that it is misleading to calculate the average yearly loss of bone mass between the ages of 20 and 70?

____

____ **(1)**

11. The diagram below shows a neuromuscular junction.

Marks

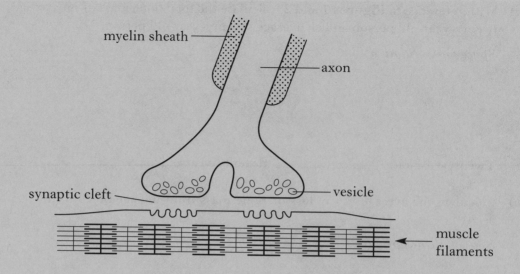

(a) How does the presence of the myelin sheath affect the transmission of the nerve impulse along the axon?

_____ **(1)**

(b) (i) What type of substance is found in the vesicle?

_____ **(1)**

(ii) Describe how the arrival of a nerve impulse at the neuromuscular junction results in stimulation of the muscle.

_____

_____

_____

_____ **(2)**

(c) (i) State whether the muscle is contracted or relaxed.

_____ **(1)**

(ii) Name the two proteins found in the muscle filaments.

_____ and _____ **(1)**

Marks

12. **Table 1** below contains a number of terms that apply to learning behaviour.
Table 2 contains descriptions of different types of learning behaviour.

Table 1

imitation	generalisation	extinction
discrimination	shaping	social facilitation

Table 2

Statement about behaviour	*Term used to describe behaviour*
Disappearance of a behavioural pattern which is not reinforced	
Production of an identical response to different but related stimuli	
Learning through the observation of others	
Production of an altered response to different but related stimuli	

(a) Use the correct terms from **Table 1** to complete **Table 2**. **(3)**

(b) Many parents use reinforcement in an effort to shape the behaviour of young children. Use an example to help explain this statement.

Example _____

_____

Explanation _____

_____ **(1)**

(c) The aim of road safety campaigns is to persuade people not to drink and drive. What behavioural term is used to describe the process of influencing people through persuasion?

_____ **(1)**

Marks

Page twenty-three

13. A series of tests was carried out to find out how quickly a student could learn to run three different finger mazes. The mazes are shown in the diagrams below.

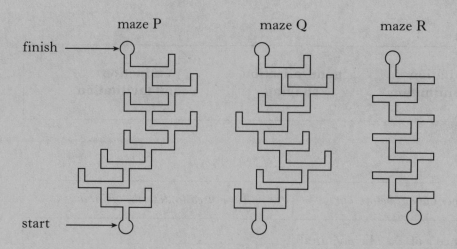

(a)   (i)   The student learned to complete maze Q more quickly than maze P. It was suggested that this was by chance.

Indicate whether you agree or disagree with this hypothesis by ticking the appropriate box. Give a reason for your answer.

Agree ☐   Disagree ☐

Reason _____

_____

_____   **(1)**

(ii)   Describe how the hypothesis stated in part (i) could be tested.

_____

_____

_____

_____   **(1)**

Candidates must not write in this margin

Marks

13. (continued)

(*b*) Suggest **three** reasons why the student was able to complete maze R more quickly than the other two mazes.

1 ____

____

2 ____

____

3 ____

____ **(2)**

14. The graph below shows changes in infant mortality in five countries between 1960 *Marks* and 1980.

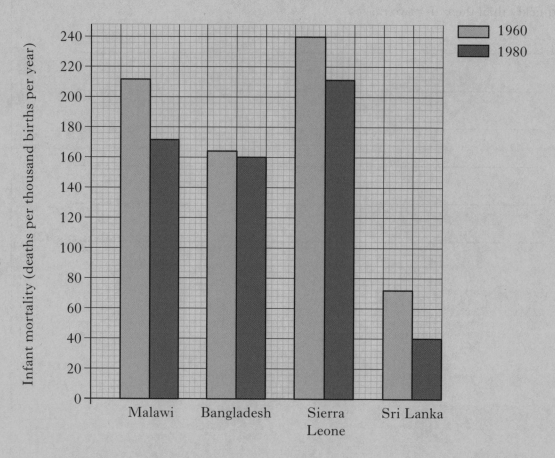

(a)   (i)   In which country was there the least change in infant mortality over the twenty year period?

_____   **(1)**

(ii)   Suggest a reason why the calculation of infant mortality may be less reliable in a country such as Malawi than in a country such as Scotland.

_____

_____   **(1)**

(b)   Calculate the percentage decline in infant mortality rate in Sri Lanka over the twenty year period.

Space for calculation

_____ %   **(1)**

Candidates
must not
write in this
margin

Marks

14. (continued)

(c) Much of the fall in infant mortality in certain countries has been due to the decline of major childhood diseases.

Give an example of such a disease and explain how humans have been able to reduce the impact of this disease.

Disease _____

Explanation _____

_____ **(2)**

(d) Name an organisation which is actively involved in the provision of assistance in countries when serious outbreaks of disease occur.

_____ **(1)**

15. The diagrams below show land-use maps of an area as it was in 1920 and as it is today.

Marks

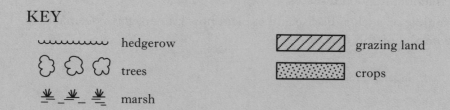

KEY

⌇⌇⌇⌇⌇ hedgerow   ▨ grazing land

trees   crops

marsh

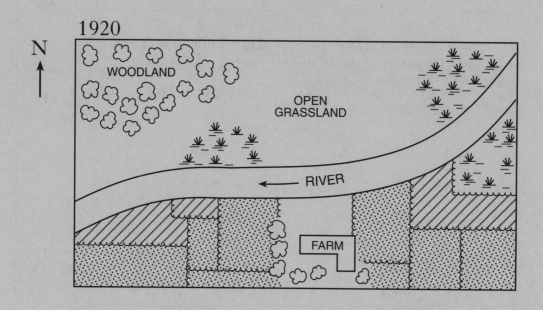

1920

N

WOODLAND

OPEN GRASSLAND

RIVER

FARM

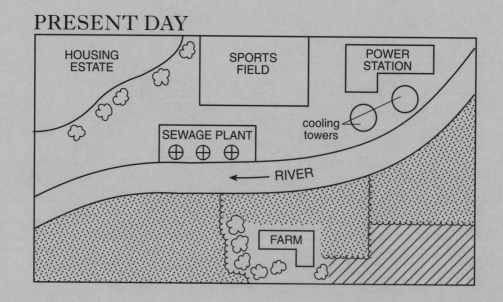

PRESENT DAY

HOUSING ESTATE   SPORTS FIELD   POWER STATION

cooling towers

SEWAGE PLANT

RIVER

FARM

Marks

15. (continued)

    (*a*)   (i)   Describe a change in the use of the area which could have resulted in a decrease in oxygen content of the river water.

                _____ **(1)**

        (ii)   Explain how this change results in a decrease in the oxygen content of the river.

                _____

                _____

                _____ **(2)**

    (*b*)   (i)   Describe a change in farming practice, shown on the maps, which has resulted in an increase in food production.

                _____ **(1)**

        (ii)   Suggest another way in which farming practice has improved food production since 1920.

                _____

                _____ **(1)**

SECTION C

Answer BOTH questions 1 and 2 on the blank pages provided.

You may use labelled diagrams where appropriate.

Marks

1. Answer **either** A **or** B.

    A. Describe how the process of meiosis brings about variation in the human population, under the following headings:

        (i)   arrangement of chromosomes; **5**

        (ii) exchange of genes. **5**

    OR **(10)**

    B. Describe the functions of the liver, under the following headings:

        (i)   carbohydrate metabolism; **4**

        (ii) protein metabolism. **6**

      (10)

2. Answer **either** A **or** B.

    A. Give an account of the principal causes of infertility in humans. **(10)**

    OR

    B. Give an account of the different methods by which information is encoded into long term memory. **(10)**

[END OF QUESTION PAPER]

Marks

SPACE FOR ANSWERS

Page thirty-one

SPACE FOR ANSWERS

Marks

Candi
must
write i
mar

FOR OFFICIAL USE

Total ☐

X009/301

NATIONAL   MONDAY, 29 MAY   HUMAN BIOLOGY
QUALIFICATIONS   9.00 AM – 11.30 AM   HIGHER
2000

Fill in these boxes and read what is printed below.

Full name of centre

Town

Forename(s)

Surname

Date of birth
Day   Month   Year   Scottish candidate number   Number of seat

SECTION A—Questions 1–30

Instructions for completion of Section A are given on page two.

SECTIONS B AND C

1   (a)   All questions should be attempted.

    (b)   Question 11 is on pages 20, 21 and 22 and Question 12 is on pages 23, 24 and 25—pages 22 and 23 are fold-out pages.

    (c)   It should be noted that in **Section C** questions 1 and 2 each contain a choice.

2   The questions may be answered in any order but all answers are to be written in the spaces provided in this answer book, and must be written clearly and legibly in ink.

3   Additional space for answers and rough work will be found at the end of the book. If further space is required, supplementary sheets may be obtained from the invigilator and should be inserted inside the **front** cover of this book.

4   The numbers of questions must be clearly inserted with any answers written in the additional space.

5   Rough work, if any should be necessary, should be written in this book and then scored through when the fair copy has been written.

6   Before leaving the examination room you must give this book to the invigilator. If you do not, you may lose all the marks for this paper.

SCOTTISH
QUALIFICATIONS
AUTHORITY

SECTION A

Read carefully

1   Check that the answer sheet provided is for Human Biology Higher (Section A).

2   Fill in the details required on the answer sheet.

3   In this section a question is answered by indicating the choice A, B, C or D by a stroke made in **ink** in the appropriate place in the answer sheet—see the sample question below.

4   For each question there is only **one** correct answer.

5   Rough working, if required, should be done only on this question paper—or on the rough working sheet provided—**not** on the answer sheet.

6   At the end of the examination the answer sheet for Section A **must** be placed **inside** this answer book.

Sample Question

The digestive enzyme pepsin is most active in the

A   mouth

B   stomach

C   duodenum

D   pancreas.

The correct answer is **B**—stomach.   A **heavy** vertical line should be drawn joining the two dots in the appropriate box in the column headed **B** as shown in the example on the answer sheet.

If, after you have recorded your answer, you decide that you have made an error and wish to make a change, you should cancel the original answer and put a vertical stroke in the box you now consider to be correct. Thus, if you want to change an answer D to an answer B, your answer sheet would look like this:

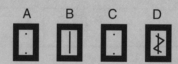

If you want to change back to an answer which has already been scored out, you should enter a tick (✓) to the **right** of the box of your choice, thus:

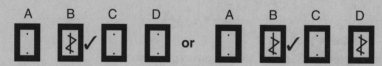

SECTION A

All questions in this section should be attempted.

Answers should be given on the separate answer sheet provided.

1. What is the name of the cell structure shown in the diagram below?

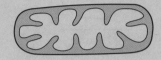

   A   Golgi body

   B   Mitochondrion

   C   Lysosome

   D   Ribosome

2. Which of the following tissues is rich in both actin and myosin?

   A   Muscle tissue

   B   Liver tissue

   C   Nerve tissue

   D   Adipose tissue

3. Endocytosis is best described as

   A   the uptake of a substance by a cell by active transport

   B   the export of a substance through a cell membrane

   C   the uptake of a substance in a vesicle formed by the cell membrane

   D   the diffusion of a substance along a concentration gradient.

4. The specificity of an enzyme is determined by the

   A   presence of an inhibitor

   B   substrate concentration

   C   state of equilibrium of the reaction

   D   molecular structures of substrate and enzyme.

5. Which of the following cells secrete antibodies?

   A   Bacteria

   B   Macrophages

   C   T lymphocytes

   D   B lymphocytes

6. The table refers to the mass of DNA in certain human body cells.

Cell type	Mass of DNA in cell $[\times 10^{-12} \text{g}]$
liver	6·6
lung	6·6
P	3·3
Q	0·0

Which of the following is the most likely identification of cell types P and Q?

	P	Q
A	kidney tubule cell	ovum
B	ovum	mature red blood cell
C	mature red blood cell	sperm
D	nerve cell	mature red blood cell

7. The mRNA codon for the amino acid threonine is ACU. What is the corresponding anti-codon?

   A   ACT

   B   UCT

   C   UGA

   D   TGA

8. Haploid gametes are produced during meiosis as a result of

   A   the separation of homologous chromosomes

   B   the independent assortment of chromosomes

   C   the separation of chromosomes into chromatids

   D   the crossing over of chromatids.

9. The transmission of a gene for deafness is shown in the family tree below.

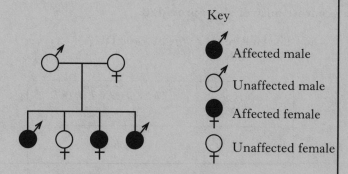

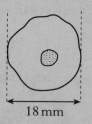

Key

● Affected male

○ Unaffected male

● Affected female

○ Unaffected female

This condition is controlled by an allele which is

A   dominant and not sex-linked

B   recessive and not sex-linked

C   dominant and sex-linked

D   recessive and sex-linked.

10. Red-green colour blindness is a sex-linked recessive trait. A woman whose father is colour blind marries a man with normal vision. If they have a daughter, what are the chances she will be colour blind?

A   0%

B   25%

C   33%

D   50%

11. Identical twins can result from

A   two haploid eggs fertilised by two identical sperm

B   a haploid egg fertilised by two identical sperm

C   a diploid egg fertilised by a single sperm

D   a haploid egg fertilised by a single sperm.

12. In a normal individual, which of the following gametes cannot be formed?

A   A sperm with an X chromosome

B   A sperm with a Y chromosome

C   An egg with an X chromosome

D   An egg with a Y chromosome

13. The cell shown is magnified three hundred times. What is the actual size of the cell?

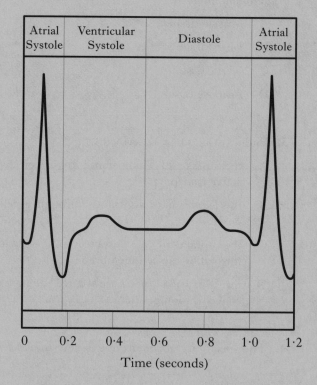

18 mm

A   6 µm

B   60 µm

C   54 µm

D   540 µm

14. The diagram below records the beat of a human heart.

Atrial Systole	Ventricular Systole	Diastole	Atrial Systole

Time (seconds)

What is the heart rate in beats per minute (bpm)?

A   50 bpm

B   60 bpm

C   70 bpm

D   120 bpm

15. Which of the events below produces the normal sounds of heart beat heard through a stethoscope?

    A   Contraction of the atria

    B   Contraction of the ventricles

    C   Closing of the heart valves

    D   Opening of the heart valves

16. A woman with blood group *AB* has a child to a man with blood group *O*. What are the possible phenotypes of the child?

    A   *AB* or *O*

    B   *A* or *B*

    C   *AB* only

    D   *AB*, *A* or *B*

17. The diagram below shows certain organs found in the abdomen.

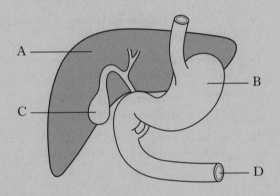

Where is bile active?

18. Which of the following correctly describes the flow of blood in the blood vessels associated with the liver?

	Hepatic vein	Hepatic artery	Hepatic portal vein
A	from liver	to liver	from gut
B	from liver	to gut	from gut
C	to liver	from liver	to gut
D	to liver	to gut	from liver

19. Which of the following pairs of compounds is produced by the pancreas?

    A   Glycogen and insulin

    B   Insulin and ADH

    C   Insulin and glucagon

    D   Glycogen and glucagon

20. The table below records the concentration of urea in plasma and urine.

	Plasma	Urine
Urea [g/100 cm^3]	0·2	1·26

By how many times has the urea been concentrated by the activity of the kidney?

    A   0·252 times

    B   1·28 times

    C   6·3 times

    D   63·0 times

21. Which of the following hormones is released by the pituitary gland?

    A   Insulin

    B   Adrenaline

    C   Oestrogen

    D   Antidiuretic hormone

22. Infants are more likely to suffer from hypothermia because they have

    A   a low surface area to volume ratio

    B   a high surface area to volume ratio

    C   a low metabolic rate

    D   a high metabolic rate.

[Turn over

23. The diagram below shows a section through a brain.

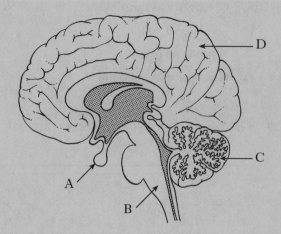

Which letter indicates the part of the brain which controls reflex actions?

24. The transformation of information into a form that the memory can accept is called

A　encoding

B　shaping

C　rehearsal

D　storage.

25. The rewarding of patterns of behaviour which approximate to desired behaviour is called

A　generalisation

B　discrimination

C　shaping

D　imitation.

26. The world production of wheat and soybean between 1981 and 1991 is shown on the graph below.

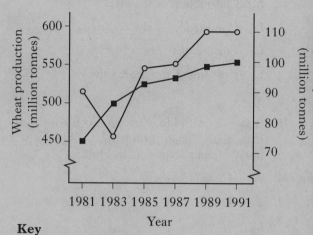

Key

■—■　Wheat production

○—○　Soybean production

Which of the following statements relating to the data is correct?

A　Wheat production is 5 times greater than soybean production in 1991.

B　Soybean production is 10% greater than wheat production in 1991.

C　Wheat production is 10% less than soybean production in 1981.

D　Soybean production is greater than wheat production in 1981 and 1991.

27. A country has a population of 50 million. What is the likely increase in population over a two year period, given a growth rate of 1% per annum?

A　1 000 000

B　1 005 000

C　1 050 000

D　2 000 000

28. Which two gases contribute most to global warming?

A　Oxygen and carbon dioxide

B　Ozone and carbon dioxide

C　Methane and ozone

D　Methane and carbon dioxide

29. Which of the following processes results in the addition of carbon dioxide to the atmosphere?

   A   Decomposition

   B   Photosynthesis

   C   Ozone depletion

   D   Nitrogen fixation

30. Rivers polluted by raw sewage have low oxygen concentrations as a direct result of

   A   large numbers of bacteria

   B   algal blooms

   C   fertiliser run-off

   D   low nutrient levels.

Candidates are reminded that the answer sheet MUST be returned INSIDE this answer book.

[Turn over for Section B on *Page eight*

SECTION B

All questions in this section should be attempted.

Marks

1. The formation of a mRNA strand on a section of a chromosome is shown in the diagram below.

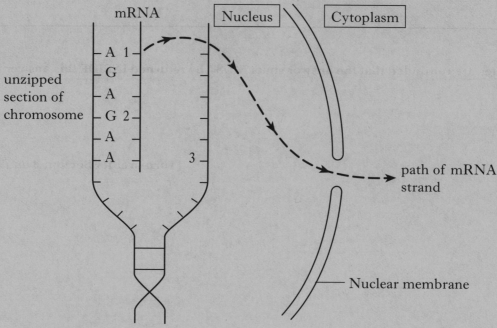

(a) Give the names of bases 1, 2 and 3.

1 _____ 2 _____ 3 _____   **1**

(b) The mRNA strand is constructed from free nucleotides.

Name the **two** molecules which combine with a base to form a mRNA nucleotide.

1 _____   2 _____   **1**

(c) Once completed, the mRNA strand moves into the cytoplasm.

What is its destination?

_____   **1**

(d) Explain why the formation of mRNA strands is essential to cell metabolism.

_____

_____

_____   **2**

Marks

2. (*a*) The table below contains three statements about two stages of cellular respiration.

Complete the table to indicate whether the statements are True (**T**) or False (**F**) for each stage.

Statement	Stages of Respiration	
	Glycolysis	*Cytochrome System*
Occurs in the mitochondrion		**T**
Releases carbon dioxide	**F**	
Uses oxygen		

2

(*b*) The diagram below summarises anaerobic respiration in a muscle cell.

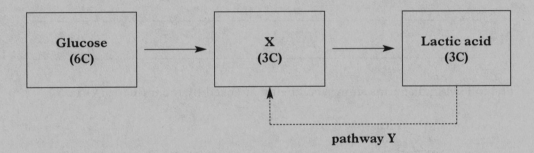

pathway Y

(i) Name substance X.

_____

1

(ii) Which substance would need to be present for pathway Y to occur?

_____

1

(iii) Why is anaerobic respiration considered to be a less efficient process than aerobic respiration?

_____

1

(iv) Glucose is not stored in muscle cells.

Name the carbohydrate which is stored in muscle cells.

_____

1

[Turn over

Marks

3. The diagram below represents the structure of the virus which causes influenza.

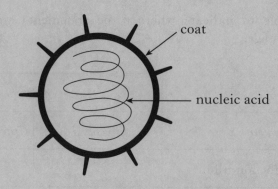

coat

nucleic acid

(*a*)   (i)   Name the substance which makes up the coat of this virus.

_____   1

(ii) Describe how a virus from an influenza vaccine might differ in structure
from the virus shown in the diagram.

_____

_____   1

(*b*)   The following diagrams show a cell being attacked by the influenza virus.

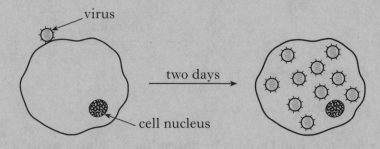

virus

two days

cell nucleus

(i)   Describe how the virus reproduces over the two day period.

_____

_____

_____   2

(ii) State how viruses are released from the infected cell.

_____   1

(*c*)   There are three main types of influenza virus.

Why are the antibodies produced against one type not effective against the
others?

_____

_____   1

Marks

3. (continued)

(*d*) The deaths in Scotland caused by influenza, pneumonia and bronchitis, between 1976 and 1982 are shown on the graph below.

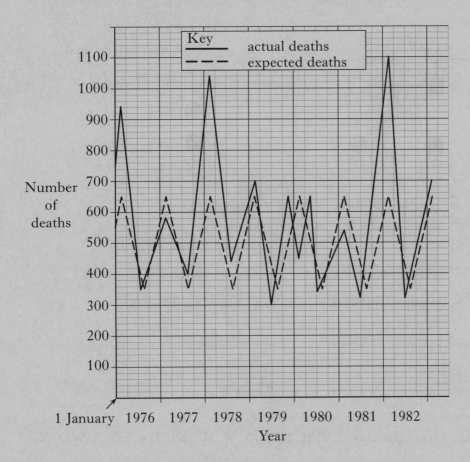

Key
——— actual deaths
– – – expected deaths

(i) What is the expected range of deaths in any year?

_____ to _____   **1**

(ii) Suggest in which years influenza epidemics occurred in Scotland.

_____   **1**

(iii) Chilling reduces the action of the cilia in the windpipe.

Explain why this makes people more vulnerable to influenza in the winter.

_____

_____   **1**

(iv) Suggest why the actual deaths in 1980 did not have the same pattern as seen in other years.

_____

_____   **1**

4. Achondroplasia is an autosomal disorder of bone growth that is caused by a gene *Marks* mutation. A person with this condition has relatively short arms and legs.

The incidence of achondroplasia in a family is shown in the diagram below.

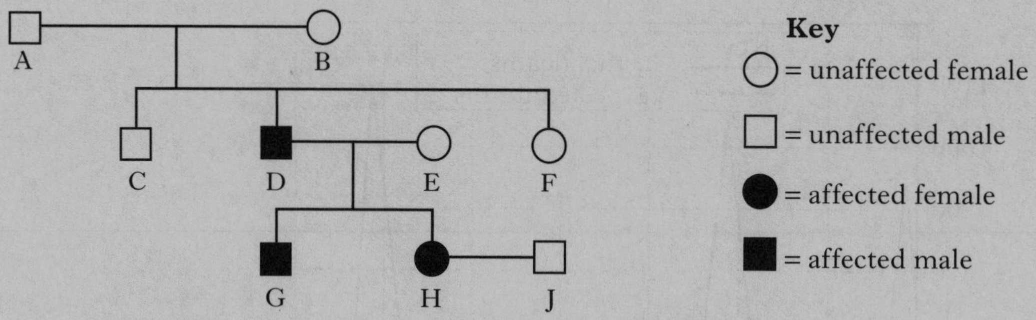

Key
○ = unaffected female
□ = unaffected male
● = affected female
■ = affected male

(*a*) (i) In this family, the mutation occurred in an ovum.
In which individual did the mutation take place?

_____   **1**

(ii) Describe a change which takes place in a gene when it mutates.

_____

_____   **1**

(*b*) The allele which causes achondroplasia is dominant.
What is the percentage chance that a child of H and J would inherit achondroplasia?
Space for calculation

_____ %   **1**

(*c*) People who are affected by achondroplasia do not produce enough growth hormone. State the site of growth hormone production.

_____   **1**

(*d*) The list below contains a number of inherited disorders.

| **Phenylketonuria**   **Down's syndrome**   **Huntington's chorea** |
| **Haemophilia**   **Cystic fibrosis** |

Select a disorder from this list which is:

(i) the result of non-disjunction; _____

(ii) a sex-linked condition. _____   **2**

Marks

5. The diagram shows a section through the reproductive organs of a man.

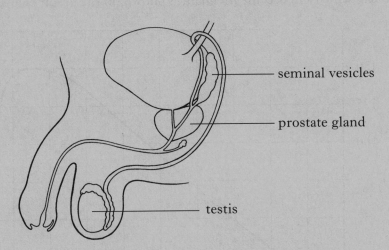

seminal vesicles

prostate gland

testis

(a) (i) State the site of sperm production within the testis.

_____   1

(ii) State **one** function of the secretions from the seminal vesicles and prostate gland.

_____

_____   1

(b) (i) During a male sterilisation operation (vasectomy), a tube is cut.
Draw a letter X on the diagram to indicate the likely position of the cut.   1

(ii) Why is the transport of testosterone from the testes unaffected by this operation?

_____   1

[Turn over

DO N
WRITI
THI
MARC

Marks

6. The concentration of progesterone in the blood of a woman over a 40 week period of time during which she became pregnant is shown on the graph below.

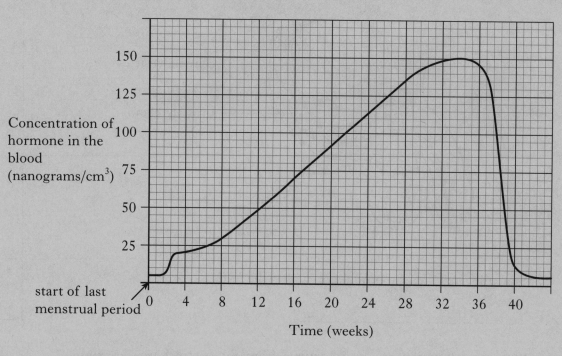

(*a*) Draw a vertical line on the graph to indicate the time of ovulation.   **1**

(*b*) Describe the changes in progesterone concentration during the first 32 weeks.

_____

_____

_____   **2**

(*c*) Where is progesterone produced

    (i) during the first weeks of pregnancy? _____   **1**

    (ii) during the later stages of pregnancy? _____   **1**

(*d*) The decrease in the level of progesterone shown on the graph stimulates the production of prolactin.
What is the effect of prolactin?

_____

_____   **1**

Marks

7. The diagram below shows the relationship between blood, tissue fluid and lymph.

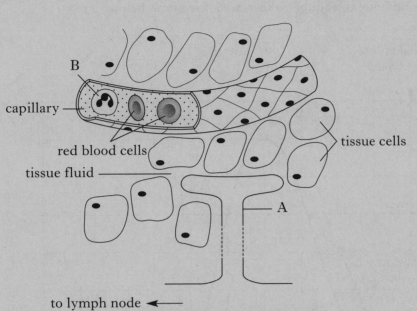

(*a*) What is the function of vessel A?

_____ 1

(*b*) Describe how the flow of fluid in vessel A is maintained.

_____

_____

_____ 2

(*c*) Explain why the lymph node may become swollen if the tissues are invaded by bacteria.

_____

_____ 1

(*d*) Cell B contains many lysosomes. What is the function of cell B?

_____ 1

(*e*) How does oxygen from the red blood cells reach the tissue cells?

_____ 1

(*f*) Explain why blood pressure falls as the blood flows through the capillaries.

_____

_____ 1

DO NO
WRITE
THI
MARG

Marks

8. The relationship between skin temperature and sweating rates of an individual in different environmental conditions is shown on the graph below.

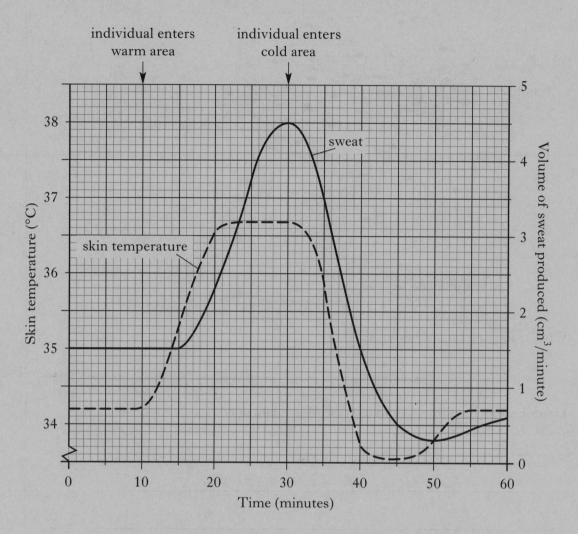

(*a*)   (i)   Express, as a simple ratio, the volume of sweat produced when entering the warm area to the volume of sweat produced when leaving the warm area.

Ratio   ——————— : ———————
                 entering warm area   leaving warm area   **1**

  (ii)   What is the relationship between skin temperature and sweat production?

————————————————————————————

————————————————————————————   **1**

  (iii)   If the individual had remained within the warm area, predict the skin temperature at 45 minutes.

——————   **1**

DO NOT WRITE IN THIS MARGIN

Marks

8. (*a*) (continued)

(iv) What evidence from the graph suggests that sweat is produced as a result of changes in the skin temperature?

____

____ **1**

(*b*) Apart from sweating, state **one** other involuntary response to an increase in body temperature.

____ **1**

(*c*) Where in the brain is the temperature monitoring centre located?

____________________ **1**

[Turn over

DO NOT
WRITE
THIS
MARGIN

9. The diagram shows how the nervous system is organised.

Marks

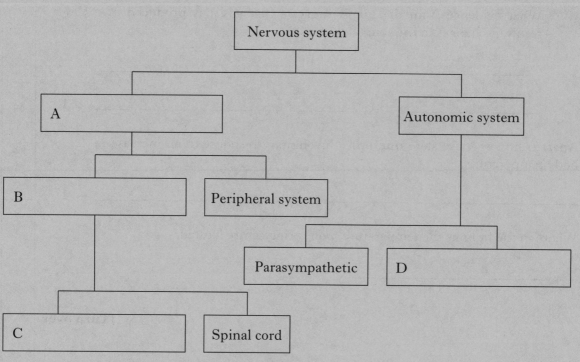

(a) Complete the diagram by entering the names of parts A to D.   **2**

(b) The parts of the autonomic nervous system are described as antagonistic.

(i) What is meant by the term *antagonistic*?

_____

_____   **1**

(ii) Explain how this antagonistic action controls the activity of the digestive system.

_____

_____

_____

_____   **2**

Marks

10. Rods and cones are light receptor cells found in the eye.

The diagram below represents the arrangement of these cells.

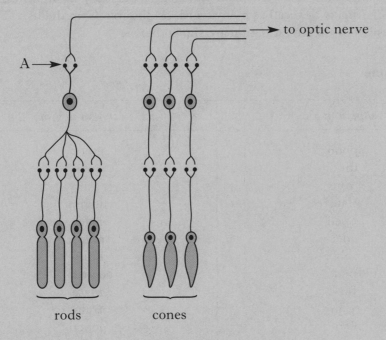

(*a*) In which region of the eye are rods and cones located?

_____   1

(*b*)   (i)   What type of neural pathway links the rod cells to the optic nerve?

_____   1

(ii)   Name gap A.

_____   1

(iii)   Explain how the arrangement of rod cells increases the chances of a
nerve impulse crossing gap A.

_____

_____

_____   2

(*c*)   The optic nerve carries nerve impulses to the visual area of the brain.
In which region of the brain is the visual area found?

_____   1

[Turn over

DO NO
WRITE
THIS
MARG

Marks

11. An experiment was carried out to investigate the transfer of information between short-term and long-term memory. Two groups of ten students were shown word lists for 30 seconds. The students then watched a video for 20 minutes, before being asked individually to recall as many words as possible from the list. The two lists and the results of the investigation are shown below.

Experiment one

List 1 (shown to group 1)	List 2 (shown to group 2)
spoon	spoon
fork	pen
knife	car
plate	turnip
pencil	ruler
ruler	plane
rubber	knife
pen	beetroot
bus	plate
train	train
plane	pencil
car	potato
potato	bus
carrot	fork
beetroot	rubber
turnip	carrot
Average number of words recalled 13·6	Average number of words recalled 7·8

(a) What feature of this investigation ensures that the results are reliable?

_____

_____ 1

(b) Why did the students recall more words from list 1 than list 2?

_____

_____ 1

[Question 11 continues on *Page twenty-one* and fold-out *Page twenty-two*

Official SQA Past Papers

115

DO NOT
WRITE IN
THIS
MARGIN

11. **(continued)**

(c) In another experiment, list 2 was read out, without pauses, to a third group of 10 students who were then asked to recall the words.

The results are shown in the table below.

Experiment two

Position of word in the series	Percentage of correct responses
1	100
2	90
3	100
4	90
5	80
6	80
7	50
8	40
9	60
10	70
11	80
12	100
13	90
14	100
15	100
16	100

[Question 11 continues on *Page twenty-two*

11. *(c)* **(continued)**   *Marks*

    (i)   Construct a line graph to illustrate the data in the table.

          (Additional graph paper, if required, will be found on page 27)

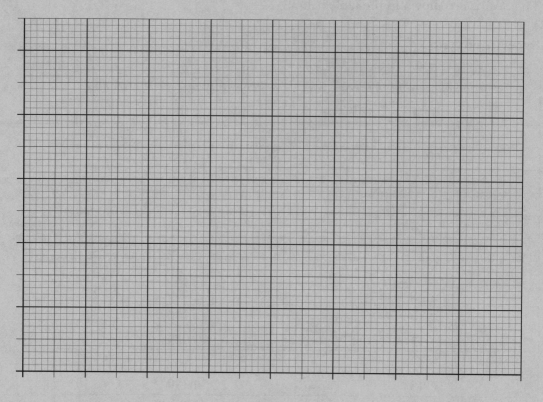

         2

    (ii)   Explain why words at the **beginning** of the list were remembered better than those in the middle of the list.

_____

_____   **1**

    (iii)   Explain why words at the **end** of the list were remembered better than those in the middle of the list.

_____

_____   **1**

    (iv)   What term is used to describe the results obtained in experiment two?

_____   **1**

(d)   What aspects of experimental design limit rehearsal in experiment one and experiment two?

      Experiment one _____

      Experiment two _____   **2**

[Question 12 begins on *Page twenty-three*

12. This question relates to causes of death in developed and developing countries in 1997.

Figure 1 Main causes of death in 1997.

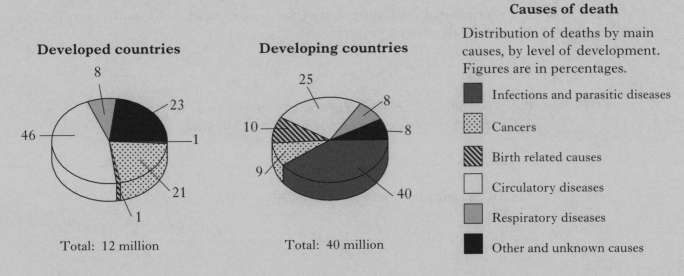

Developed countries

8

23

46

1

21

1

Total: 12 million

Developing countries

25

8

10

8

9

40

Total: 40 million

Causes of death

Distribution of deaths by main causes, by level of development. Figures are in percentages.

▨ Infections and parasitic diseases

▨ Cancers

▨ Birth related causes

☐ Circulatory diseases

▨ Respiratory diseases

■ Other and unknown causes

Figure 2 Main causes of death of children aged under three years in developing countries.

Cause of death	Specific cause	Percentage of total deaths
Respiratory diseases	Infections such as pneumonia or bronchitis	20·0
Infections and parasitic diseases	Diarrhoea Measles Malaria Whooping cough	19·1 10·4 6·7 3·8
Birth related causes	Prematurity Birth asphyxia Congenital abnormalities Birth trauma Others	9·5 8·6 4·8 3·8 7·6
Other	Malnutrition Other, including tuberculosis	2·8 2·9

Figure 3 Percentage of the population with access to safe drinking water.

Area of the world

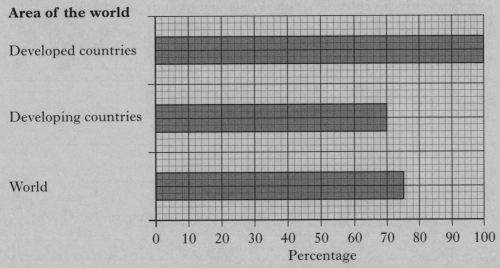

Developed countries

Developing countries

World

0   10   20   30   40   50   60   70   80   90   100

Percentage

[Question 12 continues on *Pages twenty-four* and *twenty-five*

12. (continued)

Marks

(*a*) Using the information from **Figure 1**, state the cause of death most similar in the developed and developing countries.

_____

1

(*b*) (i) Using the information from **Figure 1**, state the cause of death which differs most between developed and developing countries.

_____

1

(ii) Suggest an explanation for this difference.

_____

_____

1

(*c*) Using the information from **Figure 1**, calculate the number of deaths which resulted from circulatory diseases in the developing countries.

_____

1

(*d*) With reference to **Figure 2**, which of the following results in the greatest percentage of child deaths?

Cause of death	Tick
Respiratory diseases	
Infections and parasitic diseases	
Birth related causes	
Other causes	

1

(*e*) (i) Using the information about **developing countries** in **Figures 1** and **2**, indicate which causes of death do not significantly affect children under the age of three.

_____

1

(ii) Suggest an explanation for this.

_____

_____

1

[Question 12 continues on *Page twenty-five*

DO NOT WRITE IN THIS MARGIN

Marks

12. (continued)

(*f*) **Figure 2** shows that the incidence of child death due to malnutrition is low in developing countries. Suggest a reason for this.

1

(*g*) Using the data in **Figure 3**, suggest an explanation for the incidence of diarrhoea as a cause of child deaths in the developing countries.

1

(*h*) **Figure 3** shows that the percentage of the world population with access to safe drinking water is much closer to the percentage for developing countries than that of developed countries.

With reference to **Figure 1**, suggest a reason for this.

1

[Section C begins on *Page twenty-six*

SECTION C

Marks

Answer BOTH questions 1 and 2 on the blank pages provided.

You may use labelled diagrams where appropriate.

1. Answer **either** A **or** B.

   A. Give an account of the circulation of the blood, under the following headings:

      (i) Pulmonary circulation (through heart and lungs);   **5**

      (ii) Systemic circulation (through heart and rest of the body).   **5**

                                                        (10)

   OR

   B. Give an account of filtration and reabsorption in the kidney, under the following headings:

      (i) Bowman's capsule and glomerulus;   **4**

      (ii) Kidney tubules.   **6**

                                                        (10)

2. Answer **either** A **or** B.

   A. Give an account of the roles of lipids in the body.   **(10)**

   OR

   B. Describe how human activities disrupt the carbon cycle.   **(10)**

[END OF QUESTION PAPER]

SPACE FOR ANSWERS

Marks

ADDITIONAL GRAPH PAPER FOR QUESTION 11(*c*)(i)

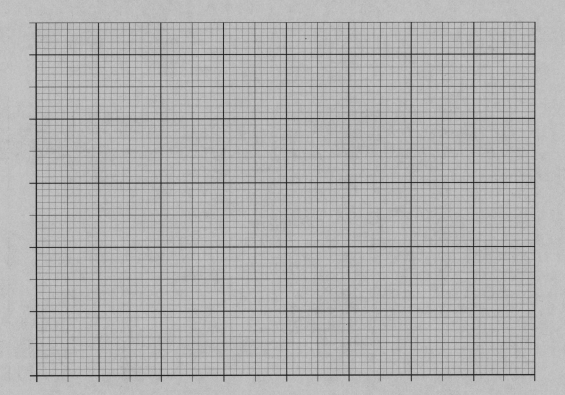

DO NO
WRITE
THI
MARG

Marks

SPACE FOR ANSWERS

Marks

SPACE FOR ANSWERS

SPACE FOR ANSWERS

Marks

FOR OFFICIAL USE

Total for
Sections B & C

X009/301

NATIONAL   MONDAY, 21 MAY   HUMAN BIOLOGY
QUALIFICATIONS   9.00 AM – 11.30 AM
2001   HIGHER

Fill in these boxes and read what is printed below.

Full name of centre   Town

Forename(s)   Surname

Date of birth
Day Month Year   Scottish candidate number   Number of seat

SECTION A—Questions 1–30

Instructions for completion of Section A are given on page two.

SECTIONS B AND C

1   (a)   All questions should be attempted.

     (b)   It should be noted that in **Section C** questions 1 and 2 each contain a choice.

2   The questions may be answered in any order but all answers are to be written in the spaces provided in this answer book, and must be written clearly and legibly in ink.

3   Additional space for answers and rough work will be found at the end of the book. If further space is required, supplementary sheets may be obtained from the invigilator and should be inserted inside the **front** cover of this book.

4   The numbers of questions must be clearly inserted with any answers written in the additional space.

5   Rough work, if any should be necessary, should be written in this book and then scored through when the fair copy has been written.

6   Before leaving the examination room you must give this book to the invigilator. If you do not, you may lose all the marks for this paper.

SCOTTISH
QUALIFICATIONS
AUTHORITY

SECTION A

Read carefully

1   Check that the answer sheet provided is for Human Biology Higher (Section A).

2   Fill in the details required on the answer sheet.

3   In this section a question is answered by indicating the choice A, B, C or D by a stroke made in **ink** in the appropriate place in the answer sheet—see the sample question below.

4   For each question there is only **one** correct answer.

5   Rough working, if required, should be done only on this question paper—or on the rough working sheet provided—**not** on the answer sheet.

6   At the end of the examination the answer sheet for Section A **must** be placed **inside** this answer book.

Sample Question

The digestive enzyme pepsin is most active in the

A   mouth

B   stomach

C   duodenum

D   pancreas.

The correct answer is **B**—stomach. A **heavy** vertical line should be drawn joining the two dots in the appropriate box in the column headed **B** as shown in the example on the answer sheet.

If, after you have recorded your answer, you decide that you have made an error and wish to make a change, you should cancel the original answer and put a vertical stroke in the box you now consider to be correct. Thus, if you want to change an answer D to an answer B, your answer sheet would look like this:

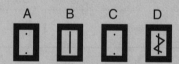

If you want to change back to an answer which has already been scored out, you should enter a tick (✓) to the **right** of the box of your choice, thus:

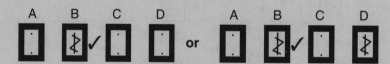

SECTION A

All questions in this section should be attempted.

Answers should be given on the separate answer sheet provided.

1. In respiration, the sequence of reactions resulting in the conversion of glucose to pyruvic acid is called

   A the cytochrome system

   B the TCA cycle

   C the Krebs cycle

   D glycolysis.

2. The diagram shows part of a liver cell with four parts labelled. In which part is most ATP produced?

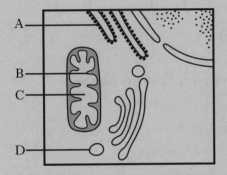

3. A DNA nucleotide could be formed from a molecule of phosphate together with

   A ribose sugar and guanine

   B ribose sugar and uracil

   C deoxyribose sugar and guanine

   D deoxyribose sugar and uracil.

4. If a DNA molecule contains 8000 nucleotides of which 20% are adenine, then the number of guanine nucleotides present is

   A 1600

   B 2000

   C 2400

   D 3200.

5. If the mass of DNA in a human liver cell is $6 \cdot 6 \times 10^{-12}$ g, the mass of DNA in a human sperm is likely to be

   A $3 \cdot 3 \times 10^{-6}$ g

   B $3 \cdot 3 \times 10^{-12}$ g

   C $6 \cdot 6 \times 10^{-6}$ g

   D $6 \cdot 6 \times 10^{-12}$ g.

6. A section of DNA has the following base sequence.

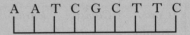

   Identify the anti-codons of the three tRNA molecules which would align with the mRNA molecule transcribed from this section of DNA.

   A AAU   CGC   UUC

   B AAT   CGC   TTC

   C TTA   GCG   AAG

   D UUA   GCG   AAG

7. The cell organelle shown is magnified ten thousand times.

   What is the actual size of the organelle?

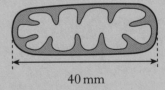

   A $0 \cdot 04 \, \mu m$

   B $0 \cdot 4 \, \mu m$

   C $4 \, \mu m$

   D $40 \, \mu m$

[Turn over

Questions 8 and 9 refer to the key shown below, used for the identification of carbohydrates.

$$
1 \begin{cases} \text{soluble} \dots\dots\dots\dots\dots\dots\dots\dots 2 \\ \text{insoluble} \dots\dots\dots\dots\dots\dots\dots \text{glycogen} \end{cases}
$$

$$
2 \begin{cases} \text{Benedict's test positive} \dots\dots\dots 3 \\ \text{Benedict's test negative} \dots\dots\dots \text{sucrose} \end{cases}
$$

$$
3 \begin{cases} \text{Barfoed's test positive} \dots\dots\dots 4 \\ \text{Barfoed's test negative} \dots\dots\dots \text{lactose} \end{cases}
$$

$$
4 \begin{cases} \text{Clinistix test positive} \dots\dots\dots \text{glucose} \\ \text{Clinistix test negative} \dots\dots\dots \text{fructose} \end{cases}
$$

8. Which line in the table of results below is **not** in agreement with the information contained in the key?

	Carbo-hydrate	Clinistix test	Barfoed's test	Benedict's test
A	sucrose	not tested	not tested	negative
B	glucose	positive	negative	positive
C	fructose	negative	positive	positive
D	lactose	not tested	negative	positive

9. Maltose is a soluble carbohydrate which gives a positive result with Benedict's but not with Barfoed's reagent. With which carbohydrate in the key could maltose be confused?

A   Fructose

B   Glucose

C   Sucrose

D   Lactose

10. The stages of infection of a host cell by a virus are listed below.

1   Host cell bursts, releasing new viruses.
2   Host cell DNA is inactivated.
3   Virus binds to host cell and injects DNA.
4   Virus DNA directs synthesis of new viruses.

The sequence in which these events occurs is

A   3,2,4,1

B   1,2,4,3

C   3,4,2,1

D   2,4,3,1.

Questions 11 and 12 refer to the information below.

The diagram shows the chromosome complement of cells during the development of abnormal sperm.

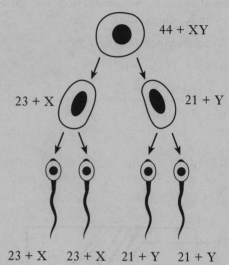

11. The diagram illustrates the effect of

A   crossing over

B   polygenic inheritance

C   non-disjunction

D   independent assortment of chromosomes.

12. A sperm with chromosome complement 23+X fertilises a normal haploid egg. What is the chromosome number and sex of the resulting zygote?

	Chromosome number	Sex of zygote
A	24	female
B	46	female
C	46	male
D	47	female

13. The colour of tooth enamel is a sex-linked characteristic. The allele for brown tooth enamel (e) is recessive to the allele for normal tooth enamel (E). The following family tree refers to this condition.

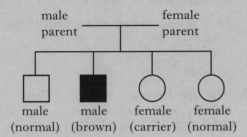

male parent			female parent
male (normal)	male (brown)	female (carrier)	female (normal)

What are the genotypes of the parents?

A $X^E Y$ and $X^E X^e$

B $X^E Y$ and $X^e X^e$

C $X^e Y$ and $X^E X^E$

D $X^e Y$ and $X^E X^e$

Questions 14 and 15 refer to the following list of hormones.

A   Follicle Stimulating Hormone (FSH)

B   Luteinising Hormone (LH)

C   Oestrogen

D   Progesterone

14. Which hormone stimulates the production of testosterone by the testes?

15. Which hormone is produced by the corpus luteum?

16. Which of the following will **not** normally pass through the placenta between the mother and fetus?

A   Oxygen

B   Minerals

C   Glucose

D   Red blood cells

17. Fertility drugs may be used in the treatment of fertility to

A   correct hormone imbalances

B   reduce the pH of the oviduct

C   stimulate mitosis in an egg

D   protect sperm cells in the oviduct.

18. The durations of ventricular diastole and systole are shown below.

Diastole   0·4 seconds

Systole   0·2 seconds

What is the heart rate for this individual?

A   60 beats per minute

B   72 beats per minute

C   100 beats per minute

D   120 beats per minute

19. In which of the following pairs of tissues/ organs, are red blood cells destroyed?

A   Liver and lymph nodes

B   Liver and spleen

C   Bone marrow and duodenum

D   Spleen and duodenum

20. Which of the following body fluids does **not** contain digestive enzymes?

A   Saliva

B   Gastric juice

C   Pancreatic juice

D   Bile

21. Which of the following results from an increase in the secretion of anti-diuretic hormone (ADH)?

A   An increase in the permeability of the kidney tubules to water

B   A decrease in the permeability of the kidney tubules to water

C   An increase in the permeability of the glomerulus to water

D   A decrease in the permeability of the glomerulus to water

22. Which of the following responses is caused by stimulation of the sympathetic nervous system?

A   Increase in insulin production

B   Increase in heart rate

C   Increase in the flow of saliva

D   Increase in peristalsis

23. A vertical section of the brain is shown in the diagram below.

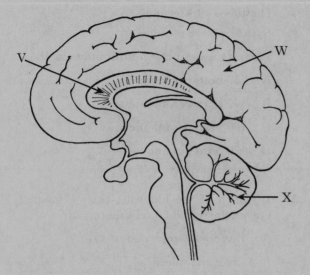

Which line of the table correctly labels the parts of the brain shown?

	V	W	X
A	corpus callosum	cerebellum	cerebrum
B	cerebellum	cerebrum	corpus callosum
C	corpus callosum	cerebrum	cerebellum
D	cerebrum	corpus callosum	cerebellum

24. Information is transferred between the two cerebral hemispheres by the

A   corpus callosum

B   medulla oblongata

C   cerebellum

D   hypothalamus.

25. A boy who is bitten by a large dog is subsequently frightened of all dogs. This behaviour pattern is an example of

A   deindividuation

B   extinction

C   generalisation

D   discrimination.

26. The development of phenotype is influenced by

A   genetic factors only

B   genetic factors and nutrition only

C   the environment only

D   the environment and genetic factors only.

27. The age structure of four different human populations is represented in the diagrams below. The bars indicate the relative numbers in each group.

Which diagram shows the population with greatest scope for growth?

A
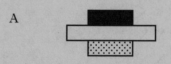

B
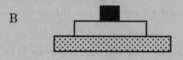

C
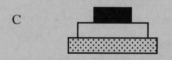

D
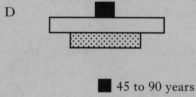

■ 45 to 90 years

□ 14 to 44 years

▦ 0 to 13 years

28. The interdependent biological and physical components in an area make up

A   a habitat

B   an ecosystem

C   a food web

D   a community.

29. What would be the effect of the discharge of raw sewage on the oxygen and nitrate concentrations of the water in a loch?

	Oxygen concentration	Nitrate concentration
A	increase	increase
B	increase	decrease
C	decrease	increase
D	decrease	decrease

30. The diagram shows a nitrogen cycle associated with the soil.

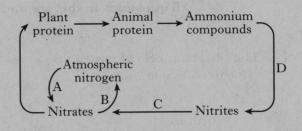

Which arrow indicates the activity of denitrifying bacteria?

Candidates are reminded that the answer sheet MUST be returned INSIDE this answer booklet.

[**Turn over for Section B on** *Page eight*

Marks

SECTION B

All questions in this section should be attempted.

1. The diagram below represents a reaction catalysed by an enzyme in the cytochrome system.

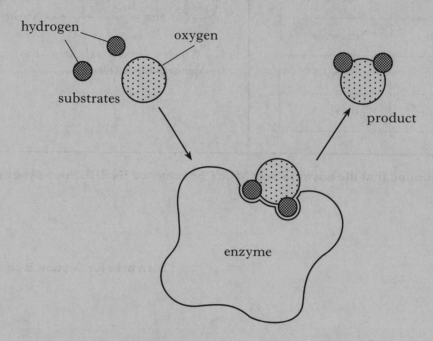

(a)   (i)   What name is given to the part of the enzyme where this reaction occurs?

_____   1

     (ii)   In which organelle would this reaction take place?

_____   1

    (iii)   Name the product of this reaction.

_____   1

(b)   Cyanide is a poison which inhibits this enzyme.
Suggest how cyanide is able to do this.

_____

_____   1

(c)   Why do many enzyme-catalysed reactions require the presence of vitamins or minerals?

_____   1

Marks

1.   **(continued)**

(*d*)   The graph shows the effect of increasing substrate concentration on the rate of this reaction.

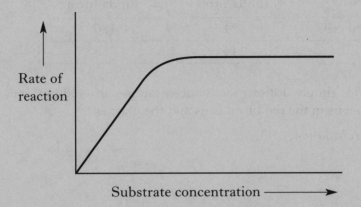

(i)   Explain why the graph levels out at high substrate concentration.

_____

_____   **1**

(ii)   Assuming that the enzyme is operating at its optimum pH and temperature, suggest how the rate of reaction could be increased at high substrate concentrations.

_____

_____   **1**

[Turn over

2. (*a*) The table below shows the relative concentrations of sodium and potassium *Marks* ions in red blood cells and plasma.

	Sodium (units/litre)	*Potassium* (units/litre)
red blood cells	24	150
plasma	144	5

(i) Express, as simple ratios, the concentrations of sodium ions and potassium ions in the red blood cells and the plasma.

Space for calculation

Red blood cells : plasma

(1)   sodium _____ : _____

(2)   potassium_____ : _____   **1**

(ii) Suggest how the red blood cells maintain the potassium concentration gradient.

_____

_____   **1**

(iii) When glucose is in short supply, the concentration of potassium in the red blood cells changes.

State whether the concentration will increase or decrease and give a reason for your answer.

Increase/decrease _____

Reason _____

_____

_____   **2**

Marks

2.   **(continued)**

   (*b*) Three samples of red blood cells were placed in different concentrations of
         sodium chloride solution for two minutes. The results of this treatment,
         when viewed under the microscope, are shown in the diagram below.

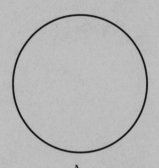   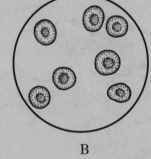   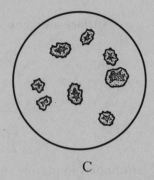

   A   B   C
(no cells visible)

   Using the information above, explain the appearance of the cells in each
   diagram.

   A _____

   _____

   B _____

   _____

   C _____

   _____   3

[Turn over

Marks

3. Antigens on the surface of red blood cells enable different blood groups to be identified.

    Four types of blood group are A, B, AB and O.

    The diagram shows antigens on a red blood cell and antibodies in the surrounding plasma.

    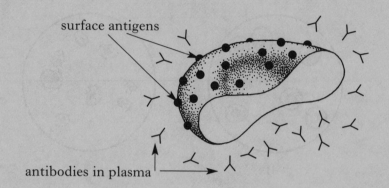

    surface antigens

    antibodies in plasma

    (a) Complete the table below to show the types of antigen and antibody present in individuals of each blood group.

Blood group	Antigens present on surface of red blood cells	Antibodies present in plasma
A	A	
B		anti-A
AB		
O		

    2

    (b) Which blood group(s) could be transfused safely into a person of blood group A?

    _____

    1

DO NOT WRITE IN THIS MARGIN

Marks

3. (continued)

(*c*) The gene for this blood group has three alleles. Alleles A and B are co-dominant to allele O.

A man, heterozygous for blood group A, and a woman of blood group AB, have children.

(i) State the genotypes of the parents.

female ____________________ ________male________ **1**

(ii) Complete the Punnett square below to show the genotypes of their gametes and the genotypes of the children they may have.

male gametes \ female gametes		

2

(iii) What is the percentage chance that a child of these parents would have blood group A?

____________________ % **1**

[Turn over

Marks

4. The diagram below illustrates the first stage of the process of amniocentesis. The fluid removed from the uterus contains fetal cells which can be grown, stained and examined.

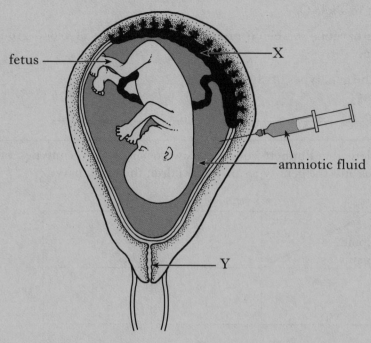

(*a*) (i) Identify structure X.

_____   **1**

(ii) Name a hormone produced by structure X during pregnancy.

_____   **1**

(*b*) (i) Identify structure Y.

_____   **1**

(ii) Structure Y produces mucus. What change occurs to this mucus during the fertile period?

_____   **1**

Marks

4. (continued)

(*c*) The diagram represents a photograph of stained chromosomes from a fetal cell.

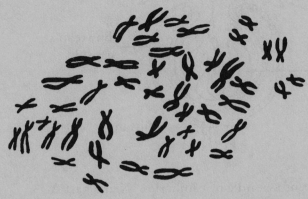

(i) The chromosomes may be cut out and arranged in homologous pairs.

Give **two** features of chromosomes which allow homologous pairs to be identified.

1 _____

2 _____   **1**

(ii) What name is given to a set of chromosomes arranged in pairs?

_____   **1**

(iii) How could the sex of the fetus be identified from this paired arrangement?

_____

_____   **1**

(iv) What other information could be obtained which would be of value in pre-natal screening?

_____

_____   **1**

[Turn over

Marks

5. The diagram below shows the parts of a kidney nephron involved in ultrafiltration.

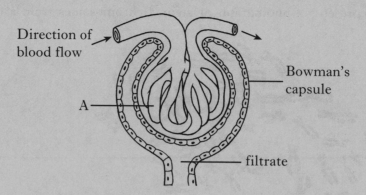

Direction of blood flow

Bowman's capsule

A

filtrate

(*a*)   (i)   Part A consists of a bundle of capillaries. Name part A.

_____   1

(ii)   What feature, shown in the diagram, results in high blood pressure within structure A?

_____   1

(iii)   Into which part of the nephron does the filtrate flow immediately after leaving the Bowman's capsule?

_____   1

(*b*)   The table shows the composition of filtrate and urine.

Substance	Mass in filtrate (g/day)	Mass in urine (g/day)
Sodium ions	600	6
Potassium ions	35	2
Glucose	200	0
Urea	60	36
Water	180 000	1500

(i)   Name the process which results in the differences between filtrate and urine, shown in the table.

_____   1

(ii)   What percentage of urea returns to the blood as the filtrate flows through the nephron?

_____ %   1

(iii)   Predict how the composition of urine would differ if the individual was an untreated diabetic.

_____   1

6. The diagram below shows the parasympathetic nerve which runs between the *Marks* central nervous system and the heart.

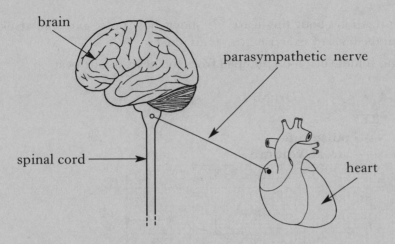

    (*a*)   (i) Which subdivision of the peripheral nervous system contains parasympathetic nerves?

                  _____   **1**

       (ii) In which part of the brain does this parasympathetic nerve originate?

                  _____   **1**

    (*b*)   (i) Name the part of the right atrium which is stimulated by the parasympathetic nerve.

                  _____   **1**

       (ii) State the effect of parasympathetic stimulation on the heart.

                  _____   **1**

    (*c*) Describe another effect which the parasympathetic nervous system has on the body.

              _____

              _____   **1**

                                                [Turn over

7. In humans, alterations in the level of exercise bring about changes in pulse rate, stroke volume and ventilation rate. The level of exercise is measured as rate of oxygen uptake.

Graph 1 gives information about the heart. It shows how pulse rate and stroke volume change with the level of exercise in an individual.

Stroke volume is the volume of blood pumped from the heart in one beat.

Graph 1

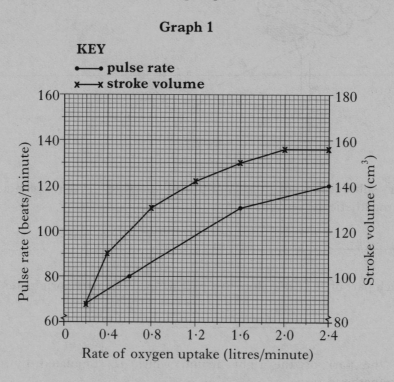

Graph 2 gives information about the lungs. It shows how the ventilation rate changes with the level of exercise in the same individual.

Ventilation rate is the volume of air inhaled during one minute.

Graph 2

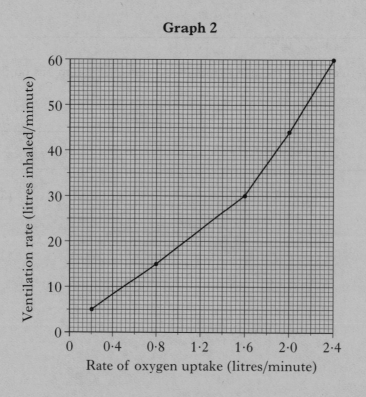

Marks

7.   (continued)

(*a*)   (i)   With reference to **Graph 1**, what is the pulse rate and the stroke volume
when the rate of oxygen uptake is 0·8 litres/minute?

Pulse rate _____   Stroke volume _____   **2**

(ii)   What is the stroke volume when the pulse rate is 74 beats per minute?

_____ cm^3 **1**

(iii)   What is the total volume of blood leaving the heart in one minute when
the rate of oxygen uptake is 1·6 litres/minute?

Space for calculation

_____ litres/minute   **1**

(iv)   From **Graph 1**, compare the pattern of changes in pulse rate and stroke
volume as oxygen uptake increases.

_____

_____

_____   **2**

(*b*)   (i)   Fresh air contains 20% oxygen.   From **Graph 2**, what is the volume
of oxygen inhaled per minute when the rate of oxygen uptake is
1·6 litres/minute?

Space for calculation

_____ litres   **1**

(ii)   What additional information would be required to calculate the average
volume of air taken in during each breath at any time?

_____   **1**

(*c*)   (i)   With reference to **both graphs**, state the ventilation rate when this
individual's pulse rate is 100 beats per minute.

_____ litres/minute   **1**

(ii)   Complete the table below by ticking the correct statement(s).

Statement	Tick (✓)
The rate at which pulse rate changes is highest at low rates of oxygen uptake.	
When ventilation rate doubles, the rate of oxygen uptake doubles.	

1

(*d*)   Name the blood vessel which carries deoxygenated blood from the heart to
the lungs.

_____   **1**

DO N
WRIT.
TH
MAR

Marks

8. Part of a neurone is shown in the diagram below.

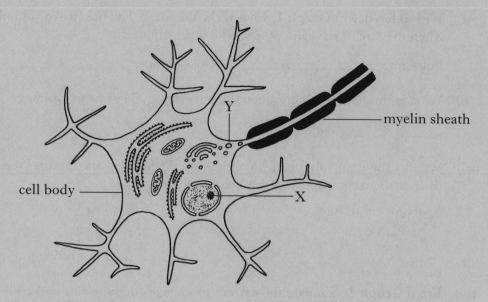

(a) State whether the neurone shown is a sensory or motor neurone and give a reason for your answer.

Type of neurone _____

Reason for answer _____

_____ **1**

(b) Name structure X and state its function.

Name _____

Function _____ **2**

(c) (i) Name structure Y.

_____ **1**

(ii) Similar structures are found in the synaptic knob. What do they contain?

_____ **1**

DO NOT WRITE IN THIS MARGIN

Marks

8. (continued)

(*d*) In the disorder Multiple Sclerosis, the myelin sheath is damaged by the body's own defence system.

(i) What effect does this have on the function of the nerve fibre?

____

______________________________ 1

(ii) What term is used to describe a disorder where the body's defence system destroys its own cells?

______________________________ 1

(*e*) Draw an arrow on the diagram to show the direction of an impulse in a dendrite. 1

(*f*) Diverging neural pathways always contain the type of neurone shown opposite. Explain how diverging pathways allow humans to perform a task such as threading a needle.

____

____

____

______________________________ 2

[Turn over

Marks

9. "Fast foods" are now very much part of the culture of the developed world.

The table below gives information about a beef burger.

Beef burger

Nutritional analysis/100 g	
Energy	1500 kJ
Protein	12 g
Carbohydrate	8 g
Fat	30 g
Fibre	1 g
Sodium	1 g

(a) A boy ate little else but beef burgers every day.

With reference to the table, explain why the boy might suffer from malnutrition but not starvation.

_____

_____

_____   **2**

(b) Increased demand for cheap beef has had an impact on the natural ecosystems of developing countries.

Suggest how this demand affects natural ecosystems and local water supplies.

Natural ecosystems _____

_____

Local water supplies _____

_____   **2**

(c) Why is the production of beef an inefficient use of land in a developing country where there is a large population to feed?

_____

_____   **1**

DO NOT WRITE IN THIS MARGIN

Marks

9. (continued)

(*d*) The carbohydrate in the burger comes from wheat.

Modern varieties of wheat have been produced by selective breeding.

Describe an improvement brought about by selective breeding of crop plants such as wheat.

____

____

________________________________ **1**

(*e*) (i) Pesticides are frequently applied to growing crops. What is a pesticide?

________________________________ **1**

(ii) Describe **one** advantage of using pesticides.

____

____

________________________________ **1**

(*f*) Genetic manipulation is now used to produce new varieties of organisms.

Describe **one** advantage of this technique compared to selective breeding.

____

____

________________________________ **1**

[Turn over

DO N
WRIT
TH
MAR

10. The apparatus shown in **Figure 1** was used to investigate the effect of nitrates on the growth of grass. Grass seedlings were grown in seven different culture solutions. The experiment was repeated ten times.

Marks

Figure 2 shows the nitrate concentrations of the culture solutions and the results of the experiment.

Figure 1　　　　　　　　　　　　　　　**Figure 2**

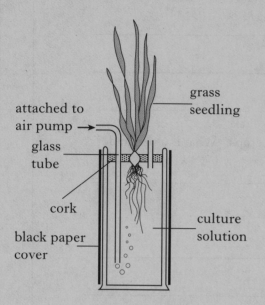

Culture solution	Nitrate content (g/litre)	Average height of plants after 6 weeks of growth (cm)
A	0	3
B	0·5	12
C	1·0	17
D	1·5	23
E	2·0	25
F	2·5	24
G	3·0	25

(*a*) Plot a line graph to illustrate the experimental results.

(Additional graph paper, if required, will be found on page 32.)

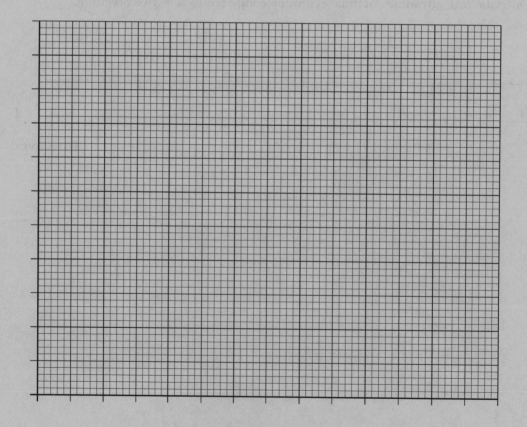

3

DO NOT WRITE IN THIS MARGIN

10. (continued)

Marks

(b) Name **two** variables which should be controlled in this experiment.

1 _____

2 _____   1

(c) During the experiment air was pumped into the jars through the glass tubes. Suggest why this was necessary.

_____

_____   1

(d) What feature of the experiment makes the results more reliable?

_____

_____   1

(e) State **one** other feature of grass plants which could be observed or measured to assess the effects of nitrate.

_____   1

(f) Predict how the results of this experiment would be different in culture solutions A, B and C if clover or pea plants had been used instead of grass plants. Give a reason for your answer.

Prediction _____   1

Reason _____   1

(g) A farmer wishes to purchase nitrate fertiliser. In what way could the information from this experiment be useful to the farmer?

_____

_____   1

[Section C begins on *Page twenty-six*

Marks

SECTION C

Both questions in this section should be attempted.

Note that each question contains a choice.

Questions 1 and 2 should be attempted on the blank pages which follow.

Supplementary sheets, if required, may be obtained from the invigilator.

Labelled diagrams may be used where appropriate.

1. Answer **either** A **or** B.

     A. Give an account of memory under the following headings:

         (i) encoding;   **6**

         (ii) storage;   **2**

         (iii) retrieval.   **2**

         (10)

   OR

     B. Give an account of immunisation under the following headings:

         (i) artificial active immunity;   **6**

         (ii) artificial passive immunity;   **2**

         (iii) the impact of vaccination on childhood diseases.   **2**

         (10)

In question 2 ONE mark is available for coherence and ONE mark is available for relevance.

2. Answer **either** A **or** B.

     A. Describe the biological basis of contraception.   **(10)**

   OR

     B. Outline the involuntary mechanisms involved in temperature control.   **(10)**

[END OF QUESTION PAPER]

Marks

SPACE FOR ANSWERS

DO N●
WRIT●
THI●
MARG●

SPACE FOR ANSWERS

Marks

Marks

SPACE FOR ANSWERS

Marks

SPACE FOR ANSWERS

Page thirty

Marks

SPACE FOR ANSWERS

Page thirty-one

[Turn over

SPACE FOR ANSWERS

ADDITIONAL GRAPH PAPER FOR QUESTION 10(a)

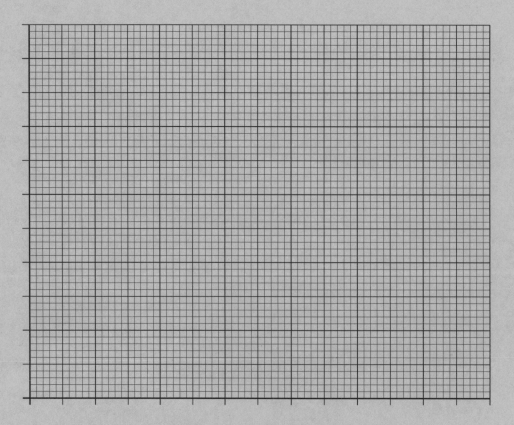

Pocket answer section for
SQA Human Biology Higher
Specimen Question Paper, 2000 and 2001

© Copyright 2001 Scottish Qualifications Authority, All Rights Reserved
Published by Leckie & Leckie Ltd, 8 Whitehill Terrace, St Andrews, Scotland, KY16 8RN
tel: 01334 475656, fax: 01334 477392, hq@leckieandleckie.co.uk, www.leckieandleckie.co.uk

Human Biology Higher Specimen Question Paper

Section A

1.	D	11.	A	21.	B
2.	D	12.	B	22.	D
3.	B	13.	B	23.	D
4.	A	14.	B	24.	D
5.	D	15.	C	25.	B
6.	C	16.	D	26.	C
7.	A	17.	A	27.	D
8.	A	18.	D	28.	C
9.	B	19.	A	29.	C
10.	B	20.	C	30.	D

Section B

1. (a) **P – mitochondrion** – provides ATP for membrane movement
   R – lysosome – **contains enzymes to digest bacterium**
   Q – ribosome – synthesis of protein

   (b) phagocytosis

   (c) (i) B-lymphocyte

   (ii) its antigens/protein coat

   (iii) by vaccination/injection of foreign antigens

2. (a) (i) DNA

   (ii) nucleotide

   (iii) phosphate, adenine, guanine

   (b) its twisted shape/helical structure/hydrogen bonds

   (c) (i) mutation

   (ii) it might disrupt a pathway/prevent it working/cause the wrong enzyme to be manufactured

3. (a) recessive
   because Jim and Ann (who are unaffected) have an affected child

   (b) Tony – Bb   Mary – bb

   (c) 50%

4. (a) *H should appear on unpaired portion of X chromosome.*

   (b) autosomes

   (c) Extra, or missing, chromosomes indicate genetic disorder (such as Down's syndrome).

Human Biology Higher Specimen Question Paper

5. (a) (i)   12µm (*units necessary for mark*)

        (ii)   1 : 10

        (iii) The ovum contains a large store of food (for the diving zygote).
               Sperm is very small to enable easier/quicker movement.

    (b) to provide energy for swimming

    (c) FSH – stimulates sperm production
         LH – stimulates testosterone production

6. (a) *1 mark for x and y axes; 1 mark each for lead/zinc points plotted correctly*

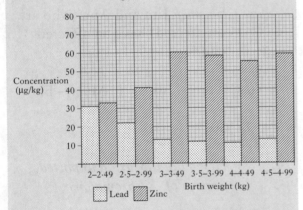

         Concentration (µg/kg)
         Birth weight (kg)
         ☐ Lead   ▨ Zinc

    (b) (i)   As lead concentration increases, average birth weight drops.
               As zinc concentration increases, birth weight increases and then is unaffected.

        (ii)   zinc may act as a cofactor for enzymes/necessary for enzyme to function properly/speeds up enzyme activity

    (c) through contaminated drinking water/lead pipes (1)
         absorbed into blood (1)
         through air polluted with lead (from car exhausts) (1)
         breathed into lungs and from there into blood (1)
         (*any two related parts*)

7. (a) A – oestrogen
         B – progesterone

    (b) *Any five consecutive boxes within 11 and 17 day period.*

    (c) ovulation/egg released
         development of corpus luteum

    (d) (i)   to permit implantation/attachment of embryo in womb

        (ii)   it does not deteriorate/it stays in place

8. (a) A – plasma
         B – lymph
         C – tissue fluid

    (b) decrease, decrease, increase, increase

    (c) Fluid is lost from the blood/energy is lost through friction with walls.

Human Biology Higher Specimen Question Paper

9. (a) (i) 37·05° C

    (ii) Heat is transferred from water to blood in arm/body.

    (iii) Corrective cooling mechanisms (such as sweating) continued to cool body.

  (b) (i) hypothalamus

    (ii) autonomic

10. (a) 10·5 kg and 5·6 kg (*units required for mark*)

  (b) 98

  (c) Bone mass increases between the ages of 20 and 33 years, so decline is by no means uniform

11. (a) it speeds up

  (b) (i) a neurotransmitter

    (ii) neurotransmitter is released from vesicle (1) and diffuses across cleft (1) to stimulate receptors on the other side (1) (*any two*)

  (c) (i) relaxed

    (ii) actin and myosin

12. (a) extinction; generalisation; imitation; discrimination

  (b) example – offer of sweets/encouragement/praise for any appropriate behaviour

explanation – reward motivates/encourages/persuades child to repeat behaviour

  (c) internalisation

13. (a) (i) *Either box can be ticked, but the appropriate reason must be given to gain the mark.*

Agree – insufficient evidence to make any other conclusion.

Disagree – maze Q is easier to learn because of its regular (2 left/2 right) design.

    (ii) Repeat the investigation with many other students.

  (b) Maze R has fewer turns to reach the finish.

Maze R has regular left/right pattern.

Maze R has shorter dead ends/with one less turn.

14. (a) (i) Bangladesh

    (ii) the gathering/registering of statistics is less well organised/communication with outlying districts less well established <u>or equivalent</u>

  (b) 44% (32/72)

Human Biology Higher Specimen Question Paper

14. (continued)

    (c) Disease – eg smallpox, polio, typhoid, diphtheria, TB etc

        Explanation – eg by introduction of vaccination programme/ better sanitation/clean drinking water

    (d) WHO/Red Cross/Oxfam <u>or equivalent</u>

15. *(a)* (i) building of sewage plant/power station

        (ii) sewage/hot water results in increased growth of plants (1)
more organic material is available for bacteria (1)
which use up oxygen (1)
(any two)

    (b) (i) reclamation of marshland/increase in size of fields/removal of hedges

        (ii) eg use of artificial fertilisers/ pesticides/better mechanisation

Section C

- *underline* indicates essential
- *(brackets) indicates non-essential*
- *OR indicates one or other answer gains mark*
- *oblique/indicates alternative*

1. A.

    (i) Chromosomes exist in matching pairs.

        Members of each pair originate from male and female parent.

        Pairs are called <u>homologous</u> pairs/chromosomes.

        During meiotic division, chromosomes lie alongside their homologous partner.

        (Homologous pairs) then migrate to equator of cell.

        They line up randomly/unaffected by the orientation of other pairs.

        This results in random arrangement of chromosomes.

    (ii) When homologous chromosomes pair up with one another they already exist as pairs of identical <u>chromatids</u>.

        Breaks occur at points called <u>chiasmata</u> on the chromatids.

        The chromatids rejoin at these points with their opposite chromatid resulting in the exchange of genes.

        This is called <u>crossing over</u>

        This results in the swapping/exchange of genes which gives variation.

B.

    (i) Glucose is stored in the liver as glycogen.

        Glucose is soluble, glycogen is not.

        So glycogen does not upset osmotic balance of body fluids.

        (The hormone) insulin promotes this process

        Glucagon promotes the release of glucose from glycogen.

        Adrenalin promotes the release of glucose from glycogen.

Human Biology Higher Specimen Question Paper

1. B. (continued)

(ii) Excess protein cannot be stored in the body.

Proteins are composed of amino acids.

Excess amino acids are <u>deaminated</u>.

Products are turned into
(i) urea and
(ii) respired/stored as glycogen.

Some proteins are manufactured by liver eg plasma proteins OR any single example of protein made by liver.

Some amino acids can be converted into other amino acids.

This process is called <u>transamination</u>.

2. A.

Infertility is failure of sperm to fertilise an egg/failure of zygote to develop.

Infertility can result from:

Males:
insufficient sperm
sperm malformed/malfunctioning
hormonal imbalance
impotence
sperm destroyed by body immune system

Females:
blocked fallopian tubes
failure to ovulate
failure to implant
fibroids OR adhesions
hormone imbalance
ovary/oviduct/uterus malfunction

Plus environmental factors such as:
obesity
smoking
alcohol
drugs
scarring from surgery
wearing of tight clothing (males)
pollution eg (ionising) radiation
disease eg sexually transmitted diseases/cancer

B.

Three stages in memorising information: encoding, storage and retrieval.

Encoding is turning something into a form which can be memorised.

Information can be encoded as sounds – <u>acoustic</u>

any reasonable example: eg saying over a phrase or number to aid memory.

Information can be encoded as pictures – <u>visual</u>

any reasonable example: eg having a mental picture of someone's face.

Information can be encoded using meaning – <u>semantic</u>

any reasonable example: eg remembering the story of a film or a book.

Encoding can be aided by (mnemonics) – memory aids

any reasonable example of a mnemonic: eg ROY G BIV.

Encoding can be aided by repetition over a period of time

any reasonable example: eg revision of work for examinations.

Encoding can be aided by organisation of material (into logical groups)

any reasonable example: eg using alphabetic organisation of names.

Human Biology Higher 2000

Section A

1.	B	11.	D	21.	D
2.	A	12.	D	22.	B
3.	C	13.	B	23.	B
4.	D	14.	B	24.	A
5.	D	15.	C	25.	C
6.	B	16.	B	26.	A
7.	C	17.	D	27.	B
8.	A	18.	A	28.	D
9.	B	19.	C	29.	A
10.	A	20.	C	30.	A

Section B

- *(brackets) indicate useful but not essential*
- *solidus / indicates alternative*
- <u>underline</u> *indicates essential word phrase/idea required*
- *spelling should be at least phonetic to gain mark, except where specified otherwise eg 1(a)*

1. (a) **1**   uracil
        2   cytosine
        3   thymine
        (correct spelling only)

   (b) **1**   ribose (sugar)
        2   phosphate/Pi (group)

   (c) ribosome

(d) to carry code for manufacture/synthesis of protein/enzyme (1)

     <u>enzymes</u> are essential/catalysts for cell metabolism (1)

2. (a) **F**(T)
        (F)**F**
        FT

   (b) (i) pyruvic acid/pyruvate *(correct spelling only)*

        (ii) oxygen

        (iii) because less ATP/energy is produced **or** because waste products contain much energy **or** because breakdown of glucose is incomplete

        (iv) glycogen *(correct spelling only)*

3. (a) (i) protein

        (ii) nucleic acid changed/damaged/altered/absent **or** virus attenuated

   (b) (i) viral DNA/RNA enters cell; viral DNA replicates; viral protein is manufactured

        (ii) the cell (membrane) bursts/ruptures **or** lysis takes place

   (c) because antibodies are specific **or** antibodies only recognise one type of antigen/virus **or** because viruses have different receptor/attachment sites

   (d) (i) 350–650

        (ii) 1975–76, 1977–78 and 1981–82 **or** 1976, 1978, 1982

Human Biology Higher 2000

3. (d) (continued)

    (iii)   because cilia cannot remove viruses/microbes from lungs (*not bacteria, dust, germs*)

    (iv)   the population is immune from previous exposure to this virus **or** there is a different weather pattern **or** a vaccination programme was introduced **or** there were different strains/types of viruses

4. (a) (i) B

    (ii)   change of order of bases **or** removal/deletion/ addition/insertion/ inversion/substitution of bases

  (b) 50%

  (c) pituitary (gland)

  (d) (i) Down's syndrome

    (ii)   haemophilia

5. (a) (i) seminiferous tubules

    (ii)   activation/nutrition of sperm/provides energy/fluid medium/stimulates muscular contraction of female tract

  (b) (i) *a cross (X) on sperm duct between testis and label-line to prostate gland*

    (ii)   because testosterone is carried in the blood

6. (a) *vertical line of any length at second week – between second and third vertical line*

  (b) level → steep/sharp rise → steady rise (*3 distinct stages described – 2 marks*) (*2 distinct stages plus correct numerical reference – 2 marks*) (*1 stage plus 1 correct numerical reference – 1 mark*)

  (c) (i) corpus luteum/ovary

    (ii)   placenta

  (d) to stimulate/start/cause milk production/lactation (*not: to produce milk*)

7. (a) to remove excess tissue fluid/to carry lymph

  (b) valves are present, which prevent the backflow of lymph(1)

    the flow is maintained by muscular action/body movement (1)

    blood pressure of tissue fluid is higher than that of lymph (1) (*any two*)

  (c) because of an <u>increase</u> in numbers/activity of white blood cells/macrophages/ lymphocytes (1) **or** because of accumulation of fluid **or** because of inflammation

  (d) it carries out phagocytosis **or** it removes/digests foreign particles/engulfs bacteria (1)

  (e) by diffusion **or** *description of diffusion*

Human Biology Higher 2000

7. (continued)

(f) because fluid is lost from the blood **or** because of high surface area/cross section area of capillaries
or because of increased friction/resistance to flow

8. (a) (i) 1 : 3

(ii) directly proportional/as one rises, so does the other/as one falls, so does the other

(iii) 36·7 °C
(*accept as low as 36·68 °C*)

(iv) because changes to sweat production <u>follow</u> changes to skin temperature

(b) vasodilation **or** relaxation of hair muscles **or** decreased metabolic rate

(c) hypothalamus

9. (a) A Somatic   B Cental/CNS
C Brain   D Sympathetic

(b) (i) working in opposition/having opposite effects

(ii) parasympathetic stimulates digestive system whereas sympathetic system inhibits digestive system(1) eg peristalsis/blood flow stimulated by parasympathetic (1)

10. (a) retina

(b) (i) converging/sensory

(ii) synapse/synaptic cleft

(iii) impulses from a number of cells come together/accumulate/are added (1) this is more likely to reach a threshold/cause impulse to cross gap (1)

(c) visual/cerebral cortex/cerebrum

11. (a) ten/many students in each group

(b) because they were organised into <u>related</u> groups/categorised

(c) (i) *One mark for both scales and one mark for plotting points. Line of best fit, **or** straight lines joining points are acceptable. Deduct one mark for: plotting to zero **or** less than 50% of graph paper used **or** x/y scales transposed.*

(ii) because early words can be rehearsed **or** transferred to LTM

(iii) because words remembered late are not displaced from <u>STM</u>

(iv) serial position effect

(d) **Experiment 1** words are only shown for 30s/video.
Experiment 2 words are read without pause.

Human Biology Higher 2000

12. (*a*) respiratory diseases

(*b*) (i) infectious and parasitic diseases

(ii) lack of immunisation programme/poor water supply/poor hygiene/ poor medical care/ overcrowding in <u>developing countries</u>

or vice versa

(*c*) 10 million

(*d*) infections and parasitic diseases

(*e*) (i) cancers and/or circulatory diseases

(ii) The children have not lived long enough to allow these diseases to develop **or** these are diseases of old age **or** children have not been exposed to smoke/bad diet.

(*f*) Most children are breast fed.

(*g*) Lack of access to safe drinking water.

(*h*) because the developing countries account for a much larger percentage/proportion of the world population

Section C

solidus / indicates alternatives one mark per line unless stated otherwise

1. **A** **Circulation of blood**

(i) Vena cava brings blood to the heart from body to right atrium

Right atrium pumps blood into right ventricle through tricuspid valve*

Right ventricle pumps blood to lungs via pulmonary artery

(ii) Pulmonary vein brings blood to the heart from the lungs to left atrium

Left atrium pumps blood to left ventricle through bicuspid valve*

Left ventricle pumps blood to body via aorta

*Atrio-ventricular (AV) valve gains one mark if other two names not used

In addition, in either (i) or (ii)

valves prevent back flow right ventricle has lower pressure/weaker than left ventricle

contraction of heart muscle is "systole"/relaxation is "diastole" arteries lead to arterioles/capillaries **or** capillaries lead to veins/venules

right side of heart deals with deoxygenated blood and/**or** *vice versa*

B. **Filtration and reabsorption in the kidney**

(i) Glomerus is a knot/bundle of capillaries

Blood (plasma) is filtered from the glomerulus to Bowman's capsule

Red blood cells *and/or* proteins are too large to pass through filter

Human Biology Higher 2000

B.   (i) (continued)

Water/glucose/amino acids/ vitamins/salts/minerals/urea pass through filter (*any three*)

High pressure due to different cross section of arterioles

High surface area for easy/ quick filtration **or** mention of high filtration volume (175 litres/24h)

(ii) Useful materials which have been filtered are reabsorbed eg much water/salts and all glucose/amino acids, but not urea (*any three*)

(most) Reabsorption takes place in proximal convoluted tubule by active transport/ requires expenditure of energy

Water reabsorbed/salts removed in Loop of Henle

ADH controls reabsorption of water

ADH acts in collecting duct

ADH makes tubules more permeable

ADH produced when there is a shortage of water

2.   A.   Role of Lipids in the Body (maximum – 8 marks)

Energy store

Useful because insoluble **or** 2× more energy than carbohydrate weight for weight

Heat insulation

Protection from physical damage eg fat pads of feet/ hands

Transport of certain vitamins (A,D,E,K)

Component of cell membranes

Diagram to show phospholipid bilayer **or** describe phospholipids in two layers

Some hormones are lipids/steroids eg testosterone/ oestrogen/progesterone

Insulation of nerve fibres

By myelin sheath

Sebum/wax waterproofing of skin/keeps skin supple/ protection from bacteria

B.   Disruption of the Carbon Cycle (maximum – 8 marks)

Plants gain carbon by absorbing CO_2 from the atmosphere during photosynthesis

Animals gain carbon by eating plants or other animals

Carbon is returned to the atmosphere as CO_2 through respiration in animals and plants

CO_2 is produced as result of increased human activity/increased population/ industrialisation eg burning fossil fuels (coal, oil and/or gas)/biomass/trees (*any two*)

Removal of plants/forests/ deforestation (to be replaced by buildings/agricultural land)

This is causing an increase in CO_2 concentrations in the atmosphere

This in turn is likely to be causing global warming/ "greenhouse effect"

CO_2 acts as a blanket, retaining sun's heat

Excess methane from paddy fields/cattle has a similar effect

This will cause icecaps to melt/ water to expand and sea level to rise

Results in major changes to weather patterns/drought/ flooding/storms (*any two*)

Human Biology Higher 2001

Section A

1. D	11. C	21. A
2. B	12. D	22. B
3. C	13. A	23. C
4. C	14. B	24. A
5. B	15. D	25. C
6. A	16. D	26. D
7. C	17. A	27. B
8. B	18. C	28. B
9. D	19. B	29. C
10. A	20. D	30. B

Section B

*solidus/indicates alternatives
(brackets) indicate desirable but not
essential*

1. (a) (i) active site

    (ii) mitochondrion

    (iii) water

   (b) It changes the shape of the
       active site.
       or It attaches to/blocks the
       active site.

   (c) They are activators/co-factors/
       co-enzymes.

(d) (i) All active sites are
        occupied.
        or Enzyme concentration
        is limiting factor.

    (ii) Add more enzyme.
         or Increase the
         concentration of the
         enzyme.

2. (a) (i)

(1)	sodium	1	6
(2)	potassium	30	1

    (ii) by active transport

    (iii) decrease
          Glucose is a source of
          energy (for making
          ATP/for respiration).
          ATP/energy needed for
          active transport.

   (b) A Cells burst because water
       enters (by osmosis).
       B Cells stay same because
       solution is isotonic/same
       concentration.
       C Cells shrink because water
       lost (by osmosis).

3. (a)

Blood group	Antigens present on surface of red blood cells	Antibodies present in plasma
A	A	**anti-B**
B	**B**	anti-A
AB	**A and B**	none
O	none	**anti-A and anti-B**

   (b) A and O

   (c) (i) female AB   male AO

       (ii)

male gametes \ female gametes	A	B
A	**AA**	**AB**
O	**AO**	**BO**

Human Biology Higher 2001

3. (c) (continued)

(iii) 50

4. (a)

(i) placenta

(ii) progesterone/oestrogen

(b) (i) cervix

(ii) thinner/less sticky/more watery

(c) (i) length/size of chromosomes/position of centromere/shape of chromosomes

banding patterns

(ii) karyo/type/-graph

(iii) by checking sex chromosomes (XY male and XX female)

(iv) whether there is an abnormal number of chromosomes

or whether fetus has Down's syndrome/ Kleinfelter's etc

5. (a)

(i) glomerulus

(ii) The blood vessel entering is wider than that leaving.

(iii) proximal (convoluted) tubule

(b) (i) reabsorption

(ii) 40

(iii) The urine would contain glucose/more water.

6. (a)

(i) autonomic (nervous system)

(ii) medulla (oblongata)

(b) (i) SAN/sino-atrial node/ pacemaker

(ii) slows/decreases heart rate

(c) slows breathing/stimulates peristalsis/constricts pupil/ decreases blood pressure/etc

7. (a)

(i) Pulse rate 86 bpm
Stroke volume $130\,cm^3$

(ii) 110

(iii) 16·5 litres

(iv) As one increases so does other.
Stroke volume unchanged at high level of exercise.

(b) (i) 6

(ii) number of breaths per minute/breathing rate

(c) (i) 23 or 24

(ii)

Statement	Tick (✓)
The rate at which pulse rate changes is highest at low rates of oxygen uptake.	✓
When ventilation rate doubles, the rate of oxygen uptake doubles.	

(d) pulmonary artery

8. (a)

Type of neurone – motor

Reason for answer

cell body at one end of neurone/

many dendrites present

(b) Name – **nucleolus** (*spelling must be correct*)

Function

manufacture of RNA/ribosomes/ribosomal RNA

Human Biology Higher 2001

8. (continued)

(c) (i) vesicle

(ii) neurotransmitter/ acetylcholine/noradrenalin

(d) (i) slows down/hinders/stops transmission of (nerve/electrical) impulse

(ii) autoimmune

(e) *arrow(s) must point towards nerve cell body*

(f) Impulse is transmitted to several points/destinations at same time.
This permits muscles/fingers to work in a coordinated way.

9. (a) Malnutrition: diet lacks vitamins/minerals/sufficient protein/fibre/sodium/calcium
Starvation: diet supplies sufficient energy (from fat)

(b) Natural ecosystems
Results in deforestation/erosion due to overgrazing

Local water supplies
results in reduced rainfall OR flooding OR silting of rivers OR nitrate/sewage pollution

(c) energy is lost at each link in food chain so the extra link/step in food chain results in energy loss

(d) increased yield
improved disease/frost/ drought/resistance **or** improved storage/flavour etc

(e) (i) A chemical which kills pests/unwanted organisms.

(ii) It increases crop yield (because crop is less likely to be eaten/damaged by pests).

(f) quicker/more precise/allows transfer of genes between different species

10. (a)

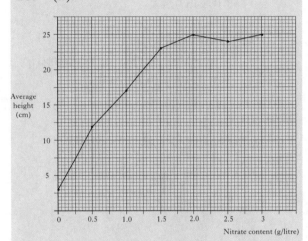

Correct y-axis with numbers and units (1)
Correct x-axis with numbers and units (1)
Correct plot by straight lines or line of best fit (1)
One mark reductions for:
  Use of less than half of graph paper. ie half-size scale
  Transposition of axes

(b) temperature/pH/volume of solution/type of seed/ light intensity/air supply

(c) to provide oxygen (for roots)

(d) the experiment was repeated (ten times)

(e) number/surface area/colour of leaves **or** length of roots/(dry) weight

Human Biology Higher 2001

10. (continued)

(f) Prediction
The plants would grow better/as well as others (at low nitrate concentrations).

Reason
They can fix/obtain their own nitrogen.

(g) It indicates the minimum amount of fertiliser required for optimum growth.

Section C

1 mark for each line unless specified otherwise
(brackets) = no marks
solidus / = alternative

1. A.

Encoding

The means by which information is entered into memory eg sound, smell, taste, visual, semantic/meaning.

(Encoding is enhanced by) rehearsal, organisation, elaboration + description or examples.

Mnemonic devices + description or example.

Storage

LTM can store almost unlimited number of items.

STM has limited capacity of around 7 items/called memory span.

More information can be held if it is chunked + example of chunking.

Excess information in STM will be displaced/ lost/transferred to LTM.

Localisation of memory in limbic system/cerebrum/ hippocampus.

Retrieval

Retrieval is getting information out of memory.

it is aided by contextual cues eg sights, smells, sounds

Serial position effect described eg items at beginning and end of a list are easier remembered.

B.

Artificial active immunity

Immunisation is the introduction of weakened/harmless form of virus/bacterium to the body.

Nucleic acid/cell contents damaged/attenuated, so will not cause the disease.

However, surface antigens are same, so will be recognised by body defences.

B-lymphocytes manufacture antibodies.

T-lymphoccytes attack cells directly.

Memory cells are produced.

So, if same pathogen invades body again, there will be faster/stronger response.

Body now has (long-term) immunity to the disease.

One example of disease for which we are routinely vaccinated. eg polio, tetanus, diphtheria, whooping cough, meningitis, measles, mumps, rubella, TB.

Artificial passive immunity

Injection/inoculation of (ready-made) antibodies into the body.

A short lived effect.

because it does not induce an immune response from the body.

Allows body time to develop its own antibodies.

Human Biology Higher 2001

1. A. (continued)

One example of disease for which this type of inoculation is used eg tetanus, rabies, hepatitis, measles.

The impact of vaccination on childhood diseases

Public inoculation/vaccination programmes have reduced death rates smallpox eradicated worldwide.

Developing countries still have high mortality due to common childhood diseases.

Examples of disease eg diphtheria, whooping cough, measles, tetanus, polio and TB.

Examples of diseases in each of three sections above must be different and separate to gain marks.

2. A.

Describe the biological basis of contraception.

Contraception is prevention of fertilisation after intercourse/pregnancy.

Fertile period lasts for a few days around day 14/mid point of cycle.

Rhythm methods of contraception rely on detection of this fertile period.

Can be detected by change in body temperature or changes in cervical mucus/mucus becomes thinner.

Hormonal contraceptives can be pills/injections/implants/ morning after which contain synthetic estrogen/ progesterone.

Pills usually taken for 3 weeks/one pill taken each day.

Concentration of hormones in blood is artificially increased.

Causes negative feedback effect on pituitary gland.

Reduced production of FSH prevents maturation of ova/eggs.

Reduced production of LH prevents ovulation.

Prolonged/regular suckling acts as a contraceptive.

Explanation/labelled diagram of menstrual cycle. (1)

B.

Outline involuntary mechanisms of temperature control.

Hypothalamus detects/controls changes in blood temperature.

Also receives information from (thermo) receptors in the skin.

(responses to overheating)

Increased blood flow to skin causes increased heat loss (by radiation/convection)/vasodilation.

(Increased) sweat production which results in heat loss by evaporation.

Reduced metabolic rate resulting in less heat production.

(responses to cooling)

Reduced blood flow to skin reduces heat loss (by radiation/convection)/ vasoconstriction.

Contraction of hair (erector pili) muscles make hair stand on end and trap a layer of air which insulates skin/prevents heat loss.

Increased metabolic rate causes increased heat production.

Increased release of adrenaline/thyroxine.

Shivering increases heat production.

Shivering is spasmodic contraction of muscles.